The Sacred Pentagraph

A Craft Work
In Five Volumes

Books IV & V

A Craft Application of Wicca
As an Occult Lodge System
And Craft Coven Organization

Tarostar V⁰

LEFT HAND PRESS
CINCINNATI, OHIO USA

Black Moon Manifesto

*It is the Will and misssion of Bate Cabal/Black Moon to
effectively manifest unique and insightful occult Works
for the esoteric community in a manner that is unfettered
by commercial considerations.*

Copyright 2019 © Black Moon Publishing, LLC

blackmoonpublishing.com

Left Hand Press is a subsidiary of
Black Moon Publishing, LLC

blackmoonpublishing@gmail.com

All illustrations in the text by Tarostar.

Design and layout by
Jo Bounds of Black Moon

ISBN: 978-1-890399-61-0

United States • United Kingdom • Europe • Australia • India • Japan

CONTENTS

BOOK IV: THE BOOK OF ELDERS

BOOK V: THE CORNUCOPIA

The Sacred Pentagraph

BOOK IV

THE BOOK OF ELDERS

INTRODUCTION

The books of The Sacred Pentagraph, I, II, III and V were composed and the system implemented while the original Elders were alive and working in organizing the Tradition.

The Coven organization, Sabbats, ritual methods and teaching guides were brought forth as their group effort, in the 1970s through the 1990s. However, over those years some passed the veil, but the remaining Elders continued to implement the system. Most of the early work was done in the Las Vegas, Nev. area. Witches and Pagans in and about the old Bell, Book And Candle Shop made up the first practicing this Tradition.

Book IV; The Book of Esbat, was only in a rudimentary state in barest outline. Through most of the later years; 1990s through the early 2000s, Tarostar and Lady Laura discussed the fleshing out of that volume and he was able to call upon the resources of The Wiccan Church of Canada and its Toronto Temple, at the old Pagan Palace of 109 Vaughn Road, to organize and perform the rituals therein offered to the Craft.

At the behest of the High Priesthood of the W.C.C., Tarostar became auxiliary clergy at the W.C.C. and was called upon to hold Craft Circles and rites at various Times over the years.

The New Moon and Full Moon Esbats in *Book IV* are the fleshed-out results from the original outline.

Lady Laura passed in the early 2000s and Tarostar has carried on as the last of the original founders of the Tradition. This *Book IV* of the *Sacred Pentagraph* is hereby given to the Craft to perform and carry forward.

Blessed Be!

BOOKS OF THE SACRED PENTAGRAPH

BOOK 1: THE COVENANT:

The Eunomia: Herein are all the Tenets and Redes of the Faith with the Laws of Wicca and Coven rules.

It expresses the conditions under which one enters the Faith and is accepted into the Craft and Coven.

The Covenant also contains the rubrics of Coven Worship.

Upon entrance into a Coven, all new members will read, sign and seal their names therein.

Therein is also The Log where all important Coven ceremonies and magic works are recorded. It also contains The Tree, which is the genealogy of the members and vital statistics of the Coven.

BOOK II: THE BOOK OF BEGINNINGS:

Herein are the Initiations where the ancient ceremonies of rising in the Degrees of the Craft are explained and given for use. All spiritual ceremonies that mark the beginning of a new phase in the total life experience of a Covener are found therein.

BOOK III: THE BOOK OF LIGHTS:

Section I: Works of the High Priest – Herein are the Coven Sabbat worship for the four Solar/Celestial Sabbats of the year.

Section II: Works of the High Priestess – The Coven Sabbat worship for the four Terrestrial Sabbats of the year.

Section III: The Manual of Exorcisms – Rituals to banish negative entities.

Section IV: Book of Elders – Concerning the Council of Elders and the Mystic Coven of Seven.

BOOK IV: THE BOOK OF ESBAT:

Herein are all the Coven Magics in full ceremony. It contains all the Full and New Moon Esbats.

BOOK V: THE CORNUCOPIA:

Herein are all the Low Magics with the Arts of Spellcraft and Divination along with the basic study course outline for teaching the Craft and development of the powers of the mind for aspirants to the Craft.

THE MOON

Being the closest of the astrological bodies to Earth, the Moon acts directly upon the rhythms of the life cycle in shedding Her powers both for good or ill.

First Quarter - Waxing. The right portion of the Moon is illuminated. When She waxes the life energy on Earth increases. This phase is used to activate, vitalize or increase.

Full Moon - Exact opposition to the Sun; total illumination.

Last Quarter - Left portion of the Moon is illuminated. When the Moon is waning life energy decreases. This phase is used to banish, conclude or decrease.

New Moon - Sun and Moon are conjunct. No visible Moon.

For Craft Esbat purposes, it is the New Moon which is the most important as far as spellcraft is concerned. It is used to bring something into being and to begin.

The Full Moon phase is used for the opposite idea in magical works.

The Moon is a signpost which indicates the prevailing direction of the life force, the reproductive energy that animates all living things – mineral, plant, animal and human.

She has a different affect at different times, depending on the Zodiac Sign in which She is passing, and the nature of the element expressed by the sign in which She passes.

To that we add the influence of the Planetary Day or Night and what aspects She makes to the other planetary bodies.

The Moon's vitality is either boosted, thwarted or channeled into specific areas of life, or away from them – all depending on Her position in the heavens.

It would be best for the Coven to have competent astrologer among its members to be able to advise the Coven Council as to the correct nature of the day or night for a particular magical work. Exempli gratia; Should a New Moon fall on a Night of Jupiter, waning Moon in Cancer, trine Saturn, opposite Neptune, what would be the primary vibration effecting a spellcasting astrologically? This is why it is important to do magic works with the most beneficial astrological energy flow possible.

In keeping with the tradition of *The Sacred Pentagraph,* this fourth volume in the series offers the Coven group Magics of both the New and Full Moons with full ceremonial.

This gives the methods in which a Coven can work its collective Will to cause situations and circumstances to change according to that Will.

However, the way the magic works is through the group being in total "one accord", as to the reason and application of the magic.

It is stipulated in *The Covenant: Book I,* that the Coven Council determines the orientation of the Coven's magical works. That is why it is imperative, to truly express the inner essence of the Craft and/ or Wicca for the entire group to be responsible for its own works and magics.

In ancient times, the temples of the old Gods incorporated within the daily ritual of sacrifice that the blood of the slain bullocks and rams be sprinkled upon the altar and then upon the community of assembled worshipers. That incorporated the worshiper within the sacred drama and made it a shared responsibility. The group enjoys the blessings forthcoming, and also shares the karma/compensation for the act. All willingly share and accept. That way the price asked for any expenditure of energy by the Cosmos is met by all and does not fall heavy upon one, or a few.

All action creates karma. Every action, either positive or negative, produces after its kind.

Every expenditure of energy, causing change in and on the etheric, must pay a consequence, also after its own kind.

Not many, today, understand these mysteries. Nor would they be willing to pay the price demanded by the Gods for their blessings and their power. Not many, today, do we find truly committed to a total religious life style in Wicca.

That is why any workings of the magics of the Craft have to accompany the adherence to Wicca as a religion and not just once every six weeks as a lark for a party.

That is why systems like this one require so much preparation and demand so much effort from the initiates.

If the correct amount of time and dedication can not be given, it is best for the Coven not to practice the Esbat cycle.

That is why these works must be determined by the Coven Council, so that all participate and share the blessings and the consequences of the use of Craft power.

New Moons of each month are only one half of the Esbat cycle. The Full Moons give us the other half. Together they present a system where, twice each month, the Coven may come together to apply its magical intention in group spellcraft, or shared community effort.

New Moons are the times for enchantments and spellcasting. Most magic practiced by a Coven is of a positive and constructive nature. The time of the New Moon is to begin projects and to promote the increase of anything desired. Health, financial increase, love, power, blessing, etc., etc., are some of the things undertaken by a Coven at a New Moon Esbat.

There are many forms of Coven magic that can be worked on a positive level at this lunar phase; cord magic, healing, making and charging talismans, in fact anything of a beneficial nature, both for individuals and groups.

The New Moon Esbats are the actual working circle of the Craft. They are where true Witches' Power is evoked and employed in spellcraft and magic.

We know that a dedicated Occultist sees the unity of mankind and recognizes all persons are aspects of the divine whole. *The Working of the Power for a positive result* should be more important than any personal feuds or personal differences between individuals.

The Craft has always been a religion of comfort and for service to Humanity. We progress in our spiritual evolution by the amount of positive energy we expend in helping other human souls lead better and happier lives. If at all possible, individual Coveners, working in a circle, must feel the same way. As Coveners,we should be universal enough, in our thinking to understand all people are part of ourselves.

A Witch must comfort, heal and bless wherever these things are needed. He/She may then quit this world leaving it better than it was.

If the Craft were not a religion of service and comfort, it would have long ago died out on the gibbets and in the flames of the "Burning Times". The fact is it did not and its services are needed more than ever today.

Mankind has a need for a religious faith which allows it to create a better life for itself and fill a spiritual vacuum created by materialistic society.

The mind of man is the creator. It creates the circumstances which manifest in our lives. A religion must uplift the spirit, solve our problems and lead us to higher truths. Then it will make of us better persons.

This the Craft in its most positive aspects can do. Hence it abides, for its essence is the soul of the world.

The Full Moon Esbats constitute the other half of the lunar cycle. However, the Full Moons are celebrated in somewhat of a different vein. Whereas New Moons are used for initiating, beginning and fostering magical themes through spellcraft, the Full Moon cycle is used to bring matters to conclusion, banish and deflate or impede.

Also, many of the Full Moons represent themes consistant with the Season determined by the Sabbat Cycle.

Some of them can be used for the mythological drama of seasonal celebrations. Not always will there be magical spells to do on a Full Moon, but mytho-drama, for the ritual cycles of the God and Goddess can be played and expressed by Full Moon themes.

The Full Moons allow us to connect with the old myths of the Gods and express those in our lives through sacred theater. I will offer some themes for the Full Moons and also give a few suggestions for magics which may be used by a Coven, if and when there may be a need.

However, it is the New Moon Esbats which take precedence for positive Craft magical works. Known authorities in Craft lore describe an Esbat as a gathering of witches for magical works, but rarely give procedures and methods.

Generally, Esbat is held and claimed as a gathering "to frolick", from the old French. Such a meaning should give a hint as to what witches would do at an Esbat.

In the old lore and in the tomes of the witchburners, usually the Full Moon Esbats are mentioned, notably by the Craft's enemies. They have been made sinister and given "satanic" intent, being a celebration outside of and uncontrolled by "Official Religion".

The High Priesthood may use these times to instruct in more advanced methods of spellcasting, or teach by hands-on practice, having the Coven participate and perform.

We are not trying to make everything binding upon the High Priesthood and a Coven Council in these matters, but offer suggestions which can be used as examples, allowing a Coven and its High Priesthood to adapt and embellish as they see fit. An "ideal" is offered, knowing full well inspiration and spontaneity are much a part of Craft works, especially at Esbat.

Esbat group working has been used by some in the past to raise the power and then allow each individual participating to use it by willing or concentrating on personal needs, each, his or her own. Such can be done, but it drains off the power and scatters effectiveness.

It is much more useful for the group to work on one problem at a time, thus combining the collective effort to bring to bear on the matter at hand.

Magic Work of any kind, other than stage theatrics brings a responsibility under the Law of Compensation. When a person sets out to strongly impress the Ether with his/her intense desire and firmly held visualizations he/she becomes a minor Creator/Creatrix of life. One must then be willing to accept the consequences and bear the responsibility thereof.

The Supreme Being/God and Goddess, bear the responsibility for the Universe as it is.

Individuals also create their microcosmic parts of the Whole, as they are.

Negativity and Dark Magics work very quickly and can leave a strong. imprint on the victims. But their effectiveness is short lived.

Positivity and Works of the Light are more difficult to bring about, but they last much longer in their after effects.

On the whole, the Universe is a positive Cosmos and a negative happening is seen vividly like causing ripples in the flow of a stream, which disrupts, but the flow eventually re-establishes itself and flows again normally. That is why evil magics eventually go nowhere and are a waste of time and energy.

The Coven entity itself must determine the type of magic spells to be cast by the Esbat Circle. The collective of the Coven Council in its wisdom is the only authority to decide the orientation of a particular working. It must be unanimous in its resolve to cast a spell by the group mind.

Only then is one-accord able to work the true Witche's Will in the Cone of Power.

In this way the whole group shares the Law of Compensation (Karma) and bears responsibility for its works. Thus, no one person or small group of Coveners will allow emotionalism to run rampant and be tempted to cast negative magics at whim. The Family is responsible for its members and the member is responsible to the Family.

There will be times when a Coven must employ the dark forces in extreme cases. The Coven Council, as determining agent, must then be in unanimous accord and willing to do so. The negative backlash will be shared by all and not fall on one alone.

Be aware that the Gods would grant the request for such, but always demand a comparable value to be given in return. Only when the benefits derived from a negative spell outweigh the price, and when the Coven Council is of one mind would such ever be done.

It would take a vote by Black Ball in the Coven Council; one white would forbid the Coven taking a negative position. (See *Book I, The Covenant*).

Acceptable Money–Making Activities Utilizing Craft Powers

- Psychic Readings for remuneration from the Public such as Crystal
- Bail, Palmistry, Tarot etc.
- Making of Talismans and Amulets.
- Psychometry, Billet Reading and Ghost Hunting, which would require Initiates of the Third Degree, or above.
- Finding lost articles by the Divinatory Arts, Water Witching and other Dowzing methods.
- House Blessings and other Blessings for Donation.
- Mediumship within the bounds of good ethics.
- Herbalism, Psychic and Unconventional Healing Practices such as Reflexology, Massage, Accupressure etc., however not to exclude conventional orthodox medicine where it would be indicated.
- Artistic Creation of Robes and Tools of Art for Craft purposes.

At least 10% of all proceeds derived therefrom should be given to the Practitioner's Home Coven, wherein he/she first learned the Craft and first developed the Psychic ability, for deposit in the Coven Common Funds. If the Home Coven is no longer active, he/she may donate to an active Coven in the District where he/she, worships at Sabbat, or where directed by an Elder of the District who would know of an active but needy Coven deserving of a Sponsor or Patron.

Uses of Psychic and Craft Power Not Permitted and Which May Bring Censure by the Coven Council

- Setting oneself up in the. Business of Sorcery.
- Casting Personal Spells for unseemly profit.
- Use of Negative or Diabolic Magics for vindictive purposes.
- Setting up shop as a. "Spiritual Adviser" utilizing notorious scams and unethical practices.
- Using the Power of Suggestion to frighten others for personal gain or to force a person to do one's bidding.
- Cursing, hexing or binding other persons for trivial reasons.
- When it is necessary to bring pressure to bear upon a person or a place, the matter should be brought before the Coven Council and possibly have the matter handled at a special Esbat
- Ceremony for that purpose, by the entire Coven.

ESBAT CEREMONY FORMAT

The points of order for a correct application of magical ceremony have five steps just like the points of the Pentagram.

I. Cast the Circle: This section consists of the usual ceremonial way the High Priesthood choose to use for a casting. In this system I offer a co-celebration of High Priest and High Priestess to erect a Cosmated Circle. This section should, after the circle is cast, also contain an invocation of the God-Forms and a Statement of Purpose for the ritual working, which includes the rational justification for the magic, or an expression of the need.

II. Combining the elements: This section is the actual magical act for casting whatever spell or work of magic to be done. For instance, it could be the application of candle work for a love spell, a healing, a charging of a talisman, a casting for money or whatever problem the Coven is working on at this Esbat. The ingredients used will suit the case.

III. Circle Dance: Raise the Cone of Power. This section is where the Coven circumambulates the Altar, or the central area of the circle where the magical act and intention have been acted out or put together.

There should be a chant embodying the idea of and for the spell or ceremony.

To invoke power, the dance, to a chanted beat, should move widdershins, as an invocatory gesture.

To banish, or impede, the dance should be deosil, also to the beat of the chant.

Both II & III could be combined at once, to have the power being raised, as and when the magic act/spellcasting is being performed.

The rhythm and tempo of the chant and dance should pick up and grow louder and faster until it reaches a fever pitch, or until the Officiant feels sufficient energy has been drawn in and is present.

IV. Discharge: This section collects the raised energy through the combined will and concentration of the Coven and through the agency of the Officiant by decree or statement/affirmation of aiming the power toward the subject of the working. The power is allowed to drain.

V. Closing: Then the circle is closed in proper ritual manner and all participants may leave the area.

THE COSMATED CIRCLE

In the Sabbat worship outlined in *Book III, The Book of Lights* of *The Sacred Pentagraph,* the High Priesthood officiated and assisted each other, The Esbat cycle, however, consists of works of group Will determined by the collective of the Coven. It is cocelebrated by two officiants, male and female.

It may be the High Priest and High Priestess together, or the Practicus and Hand Maiden together, or a High Priest and Hand Maiden, or Practicus and High Priestess. Whatever the case, a two parent symbolism needs be used. Nothing in the Manifested Universe comes into being without a masculine-feminine, or positive-negative polarity to contribute to its existence.

In this system much of the work of setting up the Altar and officiating at the ceremonies could be delegated to the Practicus and Hand Maiden as part of their training to eventually aspire to the High Priesthood.

In that case, the High Priesthood would attend and supervise, but allow the Practicus and Hand Maiden to conduct the activities with and for the Coven group. In the ceremonies which follow, the parts stipulated for the High Priesthood could be done also by III° persons.

It may be that the High Priesthood itself would take the parts relegated to the Hand Maiden and Practicus so they could assist the III° persons officiating. Use the Esbat cycle as a training ground as much as possible. That way, should a Practicus and/or Hand Maiden ever be called upon to officiate at a Sabbat, they would have some practical experience at the Altar of the Old Gods.

After all, their Initiation to III° makes them Acolytes to the High Priesthood. (See *Book II*).

Ideally a proper Cosmated Circle would alternate male-female all around the Circle area. With most new and recently formed Covens, one gender or another seems to predominate. Be that as it may, strive with time and effort to eventually build the group up to be able to cosmate a Circle properly. The Ideal of an Esbat Circle will be given herein. Covens will need to work out their practice as best they may. Some groups may meet only for Sabbat and do not hold Esbat, however, they are urged to worship the Old Gods at Sabbat and work magics at other times.

Some Covens may wish a. formal ceremonial approach to Esbat, while others would prefer a less strict practice. For that reason, knowing groups are composed of diverse individuals, no absolute and arbitrary regulations ought ever to be imposed. Magic must flow from the combined spontaneous expression of the participants acting in consensual one accord to affect the matter at hand.

Therefore, the observances described in this *Book IV* serve to offer a skeletal framework for the Coven choosing to work the Esbat Cycle. They may be employed as they are, added to or rearranged as the exigencies of a situation may warrant.

The Esbat Rites are designed to raise the Cone of Power. I will give examples as to how it is then applied.

The Coven Council will decide which Rite to use for what purpose, depending on the Tide of The Moon and the positive, and/or negative needs of a situation.

Here follows the method to erect a. formal Esbat Circle and its proper banishing. This is for the times and groups which would call for a strict observance. However, some may wish to dispense with it altogether and allow the meat of the Rite to create its own Circle as the Cone is built. See sections to follow:

THE COSMATED ESBAT CIRCLE

The formal Esbat Altar would be a combination of the symbolism of the Sabbats. in so far as the Altar Candles are concerned.

The Black and White Altar Candles from the Works of the High Priest would sit in their respective places. The Three-branched Candlestick from the works of the High Priestess would occupy the center of the back of the Altar between the two Altar Candles to signify Esbat as a co-celebration.

However, the Three-branched Candlestick is the focal point of the Rite, as it represents the Triform aspect of the Lunar Power. Luna, of all Astrological influences, affects the Earth most directly. We work by Her Tides.

The candles in the Three-branched holder could be of the color most corresponding to the reason for the Rite: (red for strength, green for fertility and abundance, etc., etc, as per standard color correspondences).

The Altar Cloth may be light or dark or colored to suit the nature of the working. Individual expression is allowed in Esbat, whereas more strict standards are applied in Sabbat. (See *Book III*.)

The Thurible, Chalice and Pentacle to hold Earth or Salt and the candle holder may be from the High Priest or High Priestess, whose

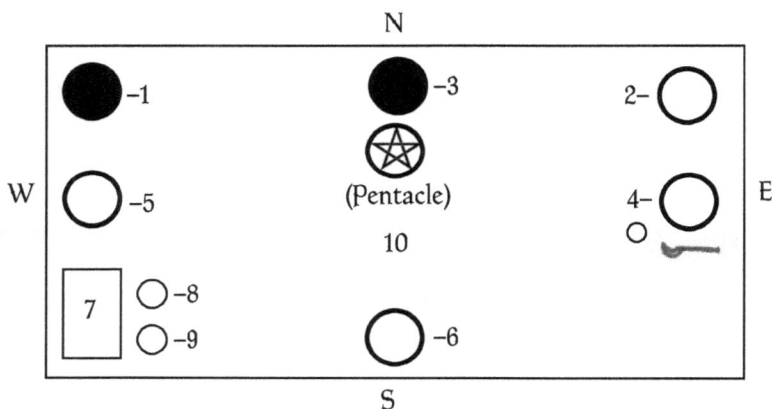

ESBAT ALTAR

1 - Black Candle

2 - White Candle

3 - Three-branched Candlestick

4 - Thurible with coals, incense and spoon

5 - Chalice of salted water

6 - Votive from the Sacred Flame

7 - Ritual Book

8 - Bell

9 - Oil

10 - Center space to hold needs for the Rite and the Cakes and Wine

Hallows are used at Sabbat, or the Coven may have a separate set of Hallows for Esbat. In that case, the Chalice should be silver for Luna.

Prior to Esbat the Hand Maiden and Practicus should set up and consecrate the Altar as per ceremony in *Book III.*

Per the diagram, positions in the circle of #1, 2, 3 and 4 are those for the High Priesthood, Hand Maiden and Practicus (should the HM and Pr be allowed to officiate, they will occupy positions #1 and 2). Position # 12 is for the Summoner, as Circle Door Warden. The other numbered positions are for the Coven members.

At the Time for Esbat, as each ritual will state, the officiants and their assistants take their respective places in the Circle area. All Coveners participating wait outside the area.

The Altar had been previously set with Incense burning.

The Besom and Staff of the High Priesthoods were handed to the Summoner as they entered the Circle area at the North-East.

The Practicus at the East Quarter, representing the Element Air, begins by moving to the Altar in the center and taking up the Thurible burning incense. Moving back to his place in the East, he steps around the edge of the Circle area widdershins, East to East saying:

Motion makes for space and time.
It is the cosmic force most prime.

Having circumambulated the Circle, the Practicus then replaces the Thurible in its position on the Altar and steps back to his Quarter in the East.

The High Priest, at the South Quarter, moves to the Altar and takes up the lit Votive Candle at the South edge and moves with it to his Quarter and steps around the edge of the Circle, widdershins, South to South with these words:

Fire comes from motion's flow.
With it the cosmos then doth glow.

Setting the Votive Candle back in its place on the Altar, he returns to his Quarter.

The Hand Maiden, from the West Quarter, steps to the Altar and takes up the Chalice of salted Water. Moving back to her Quarter, she steps widdershins West to West, sprinkling as she goes, saying:

Cosmated Circle

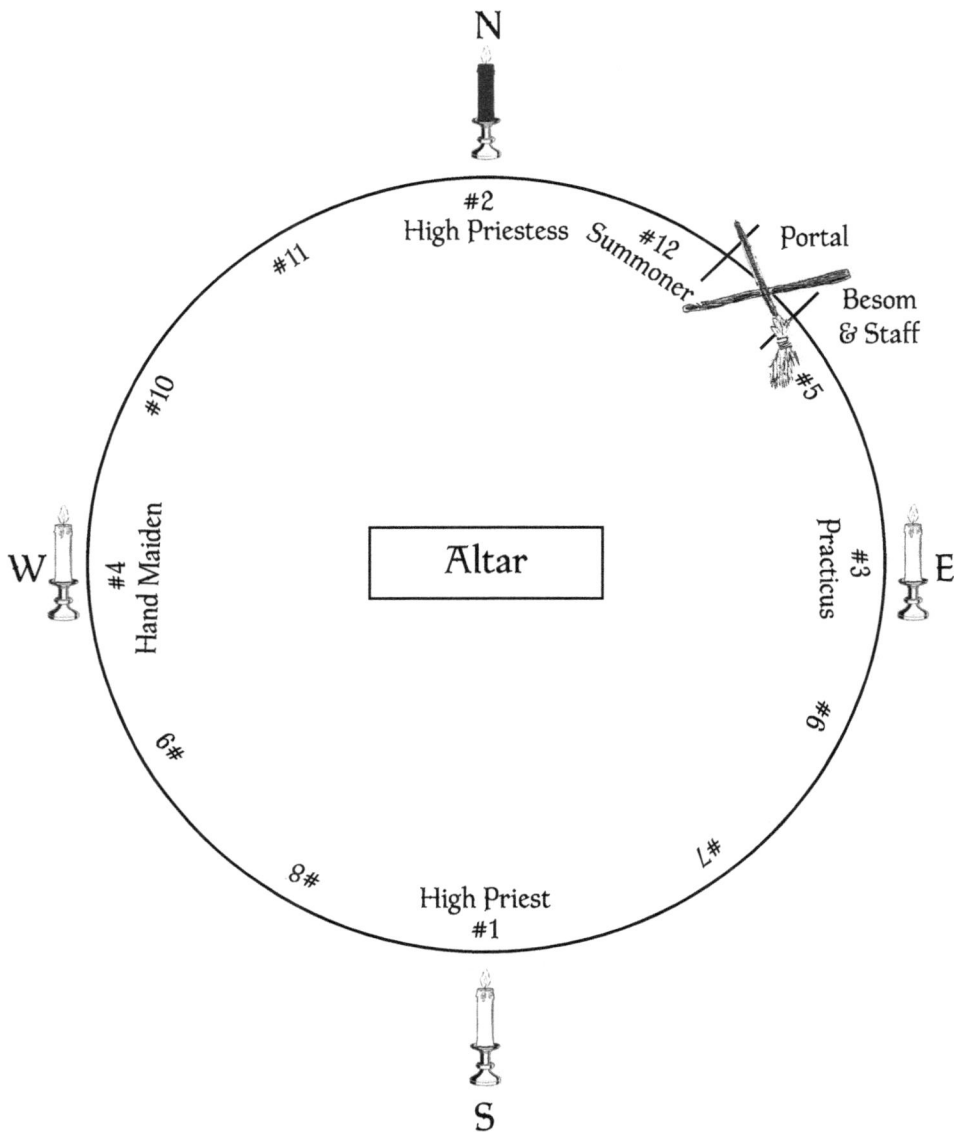

N

#2
High Priestess *Summoner* #12 Portal

#11

Besom
& Staff

#10

#5

Practicus
#3

W Hand Maiden #4 | Altar | E

#9

#6

#8

#7

High Priest
#1

S

The Officiants take their stations and the rest of the Coven
alternates around, male or female, as best as possible.

Water makes the cosmos cool,
So stars and worlds together pool.
Replacing the Chalice on the Altar, she returns to her Quarter.

The High Priestess moves to the North edge of the Altar and takes up the Paten bearing salt or earth. Returning to her place, she moves widdershins, North to North, sprinkling salt or earth, saying these words:

Solid then becomes all matter.
Across the cosmos it doth scatter.
Within which what we contemplate,
becomes our will most consecrate.

Placing the Paten back on the Altar, she takes her place at the North Quarter.

Then, the Summoner opens a portal at the North East of the Circle area with his/her Athame and bids all Coveners, attendees and participants to enter.

When all are assembled inside, the Summoner places the High Priesthood's Besom and Staff on the floor, cross-wise at the North East.

The Esbat Rite proceeds from this point.

BLESSING OF THE CAKES AND WINE

At the end of the Esbat Rite, before the Closing of the Circle, The High Priest takes up his Athame' and the High Priestess takes up the Chalice of Wine and the plate of cakes.

He lifts the blade point downward and lowers it into the Chalice with these words:

Words of Will,
thrice spoke, then still,
bind the blessing of lady and lord
bringing joy, health and concord.
He repeats the words thrice as he lowers the blade into the wine.

Then he says nothing and allows each Covener, in silence, to wish whatever private, personal need for self.

After a slight pause for the personal meditations of the Coveners, he places the flat of the blade above the plate of cakes, held by the High Priestess.

She speaks these words:

Gifts of the Gods through the bounty of earth, allow this circle to
*   expand its girth.*
Keep us well in our wiccan ways
all the remainder of our days.

She repeats the words also thrice and then pauses to allow each Covener to commune with the Gods in the silence of their inner being.

Both the High Priest and High Priestess then say:

Good Coveners in the circle of _____, accept the blessings of Lord
*   and Lady.*
To each according to Divine Will,
let thy beings with the Gods now fill.
blessed be and blessed be!

Each Covener is given to taste and to drink.

After the Circle has been closed in proper order, the High Priestess takes the remaining crumbs of the cake and the last of the wine in the Chalice out of doors and scatters them to the Four Winds with these words:

God and Goddess of the Ancient Way,
bless us by night, bless us by day.
In thy magics of the lunar tide
doth all thy goodness yet reside.
Blessed be!

(Author's Note: The Hand Maiden and Practicus may be allowed at times to perform this rite as part of their training. However, it should normally be done by the High Priesthood as the Coven parents. This may also be a short rite by itself for a communal meditation with the Gods either at a New or a Full Moon.)

CLOSING THE COSMATED CIRCLE

The Summoner takes up the Besom and Staff from the floor and stands to the side.

This Circle is closed in reverse order of casting.

The High Priestess again takes up the Paten from the Altar holding salt or earth and moves deosil, North to North saying these words:

Lift the foundations here laid down.
Let them rise from toe to crown.

Back in place, she sets the Paten back upon the Altar and stands in her Quarter.

The Hand Maiden again takes up the Chalice from the Altar and steps deosil, West to West with these words:

Wash away this circle's form.
Peace and quiet become the norm.

Replacing the Chalice upon the Altar, she steps back into her Quarter.

The High Priest takes the Votive Candle from the Altar and moves deosil, South to South, cupping the light with his free hand so it isn't brightly seen, speaking as he goes:

Darkly burns the fire stout,
to dim and flicker, then go out.

Back in place, the High Priest snuffs out the Votive Candle and sets it back upon the Altar and returns to stand in his Quarter.

The Practicus moves to take up the Thurible from the Altar and may need to replenish some incense to burn, as he steps deosil, East to East, saying:

Scatter upon the winds of space,
leaving neither spur nor trace.

Setting the Thurible back upon the Altar, he moves to his Quarter and announces:

It is finished!

The Coveners then leave the Circle area, as the Summoner hands the Besom and Staff back to the High Priesthood.

A Circle, such as the one on pg 19, would be cast on the Esbat nights when Magics or Ceremonies would be performed. When one of the playlets in the section later on is enacted, no Circle would be necessary.

However, in some of the following rites, the Cosmated Circle may not be necessary. Each Coven should work out its own preferences in that respect.

New Moon Esbats

There has been a tradition to never celebrate the New Moon Festivals on the actual Night of the calendrical New Moon. There is none to be seen in the Sky on those nights. Gathering for Esbat on the night Her first sliver of light may be seen was the measure, since the ancestors went by physical appearances, not having precise calendars. The Moon is then definitely on the increase and the Coven may work its Magics one or two nights after the calendrical New Moon.

However, in recent Times, the actual time of the New Moon can be used.

For the rituals and ceremonies which follow, the High Priesthood use them as suggestions and may opt to use rituals and rites from other traditions to variate their yearly liturgies as long as the rites are in keeping with the purposes of a New Moon.

The Ancient Rite of Turning the Silver

(For this rite a Cosmated Circle need not be done.)

- 14 white candles
- 1 bottle All Purpose Oil
- 1 large silver coin.

On the Night of the New Moon for this Coven Esbat, those who have a need to increase their financial base will gather around the High Priesthood for this Rite.

The High Priestess will light one of the candles from the Sacred Flame and the High Priest will carry the oil and the coin.

The group repairs out of doors to stand under the silver sliver of the Moon as She appears at Moon Rise. (If She has already risen, so much the better.)

Forming a circle around the High Priestess, the Coven takes up its positions and chants:

New Moon Goddess of blessed increase
we come before thee to seek thy peace.
Grant us the favor of this boon,
oh, gracious Goddess of the Moon.

The High Priestess hands the lit candle around the Circle, so that each Covener present places his/her silent intention and wish for material and/or financial increase upon it. The candle moves widdershins around and back to her hand.

The High Priest then anoints the brow of the High priestess with the oil and says:

We keep this ancient tryst with Luna
that she may bring forth our bona fortuna.

Look upon our Priestess as we pray
and let thy blessings with us stay. Blessed be.
(He passes the coin to her).

He then begins to lead the Coven in a widdershins motion around the High Priestess, as she stands in the center of the Circle holding the lit candle. The Coven chants:

Lady of this New Moon night
bring to us what is so right.
We need thy power to increase our worth.
Gracious Goddess to our word give birth.

The chant and the movement continues around as the power is built in the cone; center of the Circle. When the High Priestess feels it is at its peak, she says:

Stand and adore thy Goddess of Light,
she is with us this New Moon night.

The Coven stops in place and intently concentrates on their individual needs as the High priestess lifts the candle aloft with her right hand and begins to turn the coin over and over in her left as she says:

Lady, as thy light doth grow,
abundance upon us bestow.
Increase our worth as we ask of thee,
oh, mover of the Primal Sea. Blessed be.

She turns the coin and repeats the words nine tines for Luna.
Then the group returns into the Covenstead and she places the lit candle upon the Altar. It is to burn itself out. Each night thereafter until the Moon stands full, she lights another one to burn out.
When faithfully kept, this old tradition is said to bring abundance and prosperity to any Covenstead and/or individual in need.

THE JANUS RITUAL

New Moon in January

Performed January 1996 and 1997 CE at the W.C.C. Temple in Toronto, Ontario.

- 2 Coveners, adept at divination, to give the readings.
- 1 length of cloth to wrap around both readers.
- An incense of Benzoin, Cinnamon and Mugwort.
- 4 white or yellow candles; one placed at the left and right of each reader.

One reader would have a deck of Tarot and the other a sack of Runes, or stones.

The readers sit back to back and the cloth wrapped around them at the waist area, allowing their hands free for the castings, or card dealing.

The officiant for this rite could be either the High Priest, or the High Priestess. He would use his Coven Great Wand/Staff, she would use the Coven Besom to cast a Circle around the readers.

The Summoner assembles the Coven in the Ritual Chamber and closes the door. He/she stands close by to open it when the officiant indicates.

The readers are in place, back to back and bound together by the cloth.

The Hand Maiden, or Practicus would set some of the incense to burn and circumambulate the readers, thrice with the thurible and replacing it on the Altar.

Then, he, or she would light the four candles, sitting at the left and right of each reader.

When ready, the officiant motions for the Summoner to open the door of the Ritual Chamber.

The officiant invokes:

Janus, keeper of the past, seer of the yet to be!
Let us acknowledge the portals at the waxing of the year!

He/she simulates casting a spear through the doorway. The door
remains open during the rite.

Taking the Great Wand, or Coven Beson, the officiant
circumambulates the readers, tracing a circle on the floor widdershins
and saying:

Gods of fortune, Gods of sight,
be our helpers, here tonight.
As the times do wend and wane,
delve the depths and make it plain.
To these readers lend thy power,
that visions and portents forth may flower.
Blessed be.

The officiant steps back, away from the readers, as a Coven Bard
provides a soft musical reverie.

Each Covener, two at a time, may step forward and sit before one
of the readers and get a personal prognostication for the year ahead.

More incense can be added to the thurible and the Hand Maiden, or
Practicus would be attentive to the readers needs.

The readings are short three or four card spreads, or a casting of
three Runes, drawn from the sack at random, so as not to consume a
great deal of time, allowing each Covener, who wishes to be read by
one, or both readers.

When all those who wished have received a read, the officiant steps
forward and circumambulates the readers deosil to close the rite. He/
she says:

Gods of fortune, Gods of sight,
we thank thee for this esbat night.
A we lift this psychic veil,
let normal time and space prevail!

All may leave the Ritual Chamber and have a post-ritual social.
Casting the full ceremonial Esbat Circle is not necessary for rites

involving psychic skills employed by members of the Coven.

However, should the High Priesthood wish to do the full ceremonial, the Altar may need to be set near the Northern rim of the Circle area, allowing space for the rite to be done in the center before it.

Witches Works of spellcasting and the employ of the Art Magical would rightfully suggest usage of the full Esbat Circle to contain the raised energy and invoked, or evoked power, until it is released and sent to accomplish its intention. Works of the psychic don't require one.

Each ritual should be well thought-out in advance and perhaps even practiced, by the officiants before hand, to make sure everything will run smoothly, with minimum problems.

———————— ⟨⊰⊱⟩ ————————

New Moon Ritual for Financial Need

(Could be done for any Month of the Year as needed)

On a Night of the New Moon, or during a waxing Lunar Tide passing in an Earth or Water Sign on a Wednesday or Thursday.

This ritual calls for an even number of participants, either all of the same gender, or alternating male/female around the Circle.

- Ingredients needed:
- 2 bowls; one with water.
- Change from the pockets and/or purses of all participants.
- A green jumbo size or glass Novena "Money Drawing Candle."
- An Ace of Pentacles from a Tarot Deck.
- One Rose of Jericho; Resurrection Plant.
- t-L. C.

These ingredients would rest in 16, as per Altar set-up.

The incense to cast the Circle could be Ginger, Lavender and Sandalwood, or a traditional Money Drawing compound.

The Circle is cast and the Coven group admitted by the officiant to stand around the Circle area.

The Officiant begins by charging the green candle drawing an invoking Pentagram over it with the Athame blade and these words:

Powers of the Lunar tide,
bring thy blessings to our side.
Burn this candle to draw our need,
as we work this witchy deed!

He/she lights the green candle from the Altar votive and places the Ace of Pentacles under it, saying:

Initiate the powers of money and well-being.
According to our spelling and seeing.

More incense can be placed on the burning coals as needed.

The Officiant then places the change into the bowl with the water and takes up both bowls and steps into place around the Circle with the other. participants.

He/she pours the water and change from the one bowl into the other with a chant such as:

Luna, as thou doth grow and swell,
hear my call, clear as a bell.
From the ethers and nebulous space
bring thy fertile financial grace.
We need the money, we need the cash.
Bring it here on the dash.
Money to swell, money to spend,
money to put to lack an end.
Money to grow with thought as seed
is what we invest in this witchy deed.

Passing the two bowls to the right, the Officiant hands them to the next Witch in place around the Circle.

The next person pours the water with the change into the empty bowl and repeats the chant, and then passes them to the next person on the right.

Thus the pouring and chanting continue around the Circle until each participant has poured and chanted three times.

The bowls move widdershins around the Circle three times in all, as each participating Witch chants, pours and invests the water and coins with his/her clear visioning of the resulting better cash flow for the group.

After the last time around, the Officiant takes the two bowls back to the Altar and sets the empty one aside.

Setting the Rose of Jericho into the bowl with the water and change, to open and spread as it will, the Officiant says:

Charged water and coins of wealth
bring to us all blessings and health.

Increase our silver, increase our gold,
As we have worked with vision so bold.
Blessed power of the lunar tide,
bring the results quickly to our side.

Then the Officiant proceeds to close the Circle in the usual manner.

At that point the Rose of Jericho in the bowl of water with the change along with the burning candle can be set on the floor next to the Covenstead door as a drawing charm.

After the candle has burned out, take the water from the bowl with the Rose of Jericho and coins and sprinkle it around the Covenstead as a blessing.

Place fresh water in the bowl and keep the Rose of Jericho moist and fresh until the financial boon manifests.

During that period after the casting of the spell there will usually ensue discussions of ways to budget and better employ the group's finances and ideas and opportunities will present themselves for bringing the needed cash flow.

The discussions are not "negative", but a healing catharsis to help the group better handle the financial needs; a healing crisis.

The ritual shakes up the group lethargy and gets the ball rolling to a better and brighter financial future.

Running a Coven, especially in this Tradition, can be rather expensive. High Priests' robes and jewels, supplies, Coven expenses, Sabbat and Esbat meals, etc., etc., should not be expected to be the burden of the High Priesthood alone.

Coven dues are provided for, as seen in *Book I, The Covenant* and various other money making activities can be employed by the group.

This is why financial spells, from diverse traditions are offered to use as an Esbat Rite, when needed.

Naturally, all accumulated funds from Coven activity would go into the Coven Common Funds and be accounted for by the Second Scribe, as that office is required to do, per The Covenant.

A Witch's Reading

by Tarostar

New Moon Esbat. A rite to gather psychic insight from the Coven.

Sister witch and brother too,
Tell me what I am to do.
I seek thy redes, I search thy runes
To find my Coven's precious boons.
Scry my face and scry my form
That knowledge in droves to thee may swarm.
Witches know and witches show
The omens which upon the wind do blow.
By "the pricking of thy thumbs",
Tell me of what here comes.
By the candles burning bright,
Give thy word unto the night.
By the incense of mystic scent,
Tell me of the Gods' intent.
Oh, brother witch and sister too, I seek the Wiccan Way so true.

A Witch's Reading

Suggested for February New Moon

On a night of the New Moon, gather for esbat and cast the Circle in the usual manner.

To open the heart of the ceremony, after all Coveners have assembled inside the Circle, have a small cauldron burning coals and mugwort.

Place around the cauldron nine white candles anointed with Moon Goddess or Gardenia Oil.

Have one Covener, the one to be read, sit facing North before the cauldron in the center of the Circle.

All other Coveners sit semi-circle around the one facing to the South, looking directly at the one Covener to be read, through the misty mugwort fumes.

Both the High Priest and High Priestess chant:

Witches all do gather around.
Cogitate without a sound.
Read thy (brother/sister) here,
giving thy insight both good or drear.

All Coveners then chant:

We see, we see, we truly see, that which comes on wings of air,
that which comes both ill or fair.
We tell, we tell, we truly tell, be it blessed or be it fell.
Let the Gods illuminate our mind,
that in our reading truth we'll find.

All then silently sit and focus on the eyes of the Covener being read, or on a part of the body, or on the space or wall behind him or her.

Slowly, out of the silence, impressions will come. Each one is to verbalize the impressions as they press upon the mind.

No doctoring, nor rationalizations should be allowed to change the immediate first impressions.

Each witch present should speak out the impressions as they are urged into the consciousness, freely, without any attempt to impress or appear knowledgeable. It is a free association of the vibrations for the one being read.

There can be an order to start, such as going from one side of the semi-circle to the other, allowing each witch to verbalize his/her psychic impressions as they come.

However it is done, it is a psychic reading giving the individual the benefit of the group consciousness, freely, without cause to try and impress any specific ideas onto the one being read. He/she must be allowed to interpret as he/she will.*

The impressions can be written down by each witch receiving them, to be discussed later and entered into the log.

Impressions come in short phrases, or in simple ideas, which may appear to have no rhyme or reason. They are symbols from the psychic.

That is why it may be necessary to have a discussion period to allow all input into interpretation along with the one read, after the circle is closed.

When the energy feels to be on the wane, the High Priesthood together will chant:

Thank thee, thank tree, thank thee all.
Let normal time and space here fall.
The veil doth close and seal the channel shut.
By this chant the lines be cut:
New Moon by thy sliver so white,
we thank thee on this esbat night.
For thy gift of the second sight,
we bless thee as thou groweth in light.

The Ceremony of The Cakes and Wine would then follow to bless the rite before proper closing of the Circle.

This New Moon Esbat can be done whenever a Covener has a serious need for the collective input of the entire Coven for a heavy problem.

Highly effective it is when only the officiants know what the Covener's problem may be, but the rest of the group do not.

That way the true insight of the collective group mind comes to bear. However, it should only be done Saw once a year for any individual Covener. That way, one Covener does not hog the lime light and become a center stage attraction, depriving others of the benefit at other Esbats.

* Attempts to propagandize, or influence a person to a specific mode of action or belief, by any conscious directing of the impressions by anyone, High Priesthood or Coven Officers, or individual Coveners, will void the rite, as it deprives the Gods of an open channel. That will bring its own consequences in their own good time.

WISHES IN THE FLAME

A Ritual Chant by the Author
(Could be used in the rite to follow.)

Oh, burning candle of the Moon,
Short thy life and gone too soon.
Dressed with oil of the Lunar Tide,
Burn to bring wishes to my side.
Lit to blaze an the New Moon's Night,
Disspell all darkness by thy light.
I wish upon the candle flame,
And ask for blessings in the Goddess's Name.
An increase of love, an increase of joys,
An end to an enemy's plots and ploys.
Things to wish into the Things to wish into the fire
Are all the wealth of thy heart's desire.
Burn for me, as thou art lit,
Bringing my wish as The Lady sees fit.
Oh, burning candle, so tall and white, '
I ask only what would be right.
I wish, I wish, I really need
This thought I set to become pure deed.
Thoughts are things which wander and wend.
But very potent, when with flame I send.
I vision in thy flame, brightly burning,
The World according to my Will new turning.
I see my wish as very real.
All thereto will now congeal.
Oh, burning candle, flash and flicker.
As thou burneth away, my wish becometh thicker!

WISHES IN THE FLAME RITUAL

New Moon Esbat for February after Candlemas

One white candle inscribed with a Moon Crescent, a Pentagram and a symbol of the Element for the purpose: Air, Water, Fire, Earth.

Use a Moon Goddess or Lotus Oil for anointing and charging the candle.

Vision the wish clearly as the oil is rubbed on.

The Officiant casts the Circle as per usual method and assembles the Coven inside.

The officiant recites the chant above as he/she dresses and charges the candle. He/she sets a bit of Sandalwood incense to burn and lights the candle, set in the center of the Altar.

The Coven begins to circle the Altar widdershins if the wish is to attract a boon, or deosil if to banish a negative.

The Officiant repeats the chant or a shorter version of it over and over, faster and faster as the Coven's circling heats up, each member concentrating on the wish being fulfilled in the Present.

When the power drawn in feels to be at its height, the Officiant calls to order and all repeat:

It is done!

The Circle is then closed in the usual manner after the Cakes and Wine.

A Witch's Tarot Spread Ritual

New Moon of March

(Any standard Tarot Deck favored by the Officiant)

A casting of the cards in four pentagrams for a reading of the planes of being that most concern individuals and circumstances.

Arrange the Altar to face North and set up the candles, chalice of water, incense and Earth symbol as shown in the diagram that follows.

A red candle will stand near the West edge of the Altar representing Fire of Spirit. A chalice of clear water rests between it and the blue candle as a symbol of mentality.

In the center is the Thurible to burn a Mercurial Incense. To the right of the Thurible stands a green candle for emotional health. Next to that is the symbolic Earth Element; the Altar Pentacle or a small dish of salt. A brown or yellow candle completes the Altar set up representing the physical plane at the East edge of the Altar.

The Reader/Officiant stands at the South of the Altar facing North. The pack of Tarot Cards rests near the Southern edge of the Altar directly in front of the Reader. A small candle lighted from the Sacred Flame in the Covenstead Sanctum sits to the North of the Tarot Deck.

The Esbat Circle is cast in the normal way the Coven uses for Esbat. When all is ready, begin the reading thus:

Knock five times upon the Altar to summon the forces of impartial Justice; X X X X X.

Light the four candles from the small candle at the South of the Altar and the coals in the Thurible and say:

That which seers mark as fate,
that which deals with love or hate,
that which may be small or great,
let this rite now illuminate.

Sprinkle some of the Mercurial Incense on the coals and continue:

The planes of being summoned here,
forces from the nether world,
neatly in the cards appear.

The small candle at the South is put back in place.

The Reader consecrates the Tarot Deck for this rite thus:

He/she sprinkles the deck with a few drops of water from the Chalice and touches the deck to the Earth symbol, the Altar Pentacle or the dish of salt as he/she concentrates on cleansing them of any previous associations. Then, the deck is passed thrice through the incense smoke and once over each candle on the Altar as he/she dedicates the deck mentally to the work at hand.

The Reader then recites this prayer while holding the deck above the Altar:

Powers of impartial truth, divinitory elements show forth we pray,
to our enlightenment, that which, for us this day/night, in honest
decipherment, an answer is given, as the cards fall where they may.
God and Goddess, Supreme and Supernal head of all, read the
innermost needs of our thoughts and show us a sign. come to our
call ...

He/she meditates on the question or circumstance upon which illumination is sought for a full sixty seconds. Then, passes the cards thrice again through the incense smoke and once again over the candles on the Altar and says:

I, _____, Priest(ess) and Witch, do open this Sacred Book
of seeing. Let my hand be guided by the spirit of impartial truth.
So be it done!

He/she shuffles the cards and mixes them well maintaining silence until time to read and interpret.

When the cards are thoroughly mixed, one is laid to the North of the red candle face down.

The second to the South-West of that candle. The third to the East of the candle. The fourth to the West of the candle and the fifth to the South-East as shown in the diagram that follows. They must be dealt from the top of the deck.

The remaining cards are mixed and shuffled a second time and the same done around the blue candle in the exact order as before. They are shuffled and mixed a third time and arranged around the green candle. This is repeated a fourth time and placed around the brown or yellow candle. This gives five cards arranged around the four candles on the Altar, 20 cards dealt out.

The Officiant shuffles and mixes the remaining cards concentrating on obtaining the final answer to the lay-out and then places the twenty-first card to the South of the Thurible standing in the center of the Altar. The remaining cards are set back in place from the start.

Beginning with the five cards around the red candle, they are turned over in the order 1 through 5 being careful not to reverse them from the way they have been dealt out. They are read and interpreted from a spiritual standpoint.

Moving to the cards around the blue candle, repeat the process reading them for their meaning in the mental realm.

Those around the green candle are read for their illumination and commentary on the emotional level affecting the question, or the circumstances involved.

The last set of cards, around the brown or yellow candle are read as to the results and consequences of the previous three sets and effect on the physical plane.

The twenty-first card is turned up and read as the final results and answer.

If the cards are approached and handled this way in a respectful manner, they will give serious answers

This spread is for questions of great import to individuals or Covens and should not be used for frivolous matters where one of the less complicated spreads would do.

The date and phase of the Moon and card sequence should all be recorded for future reference.

After the reading and interpretation are given and recorded, the Officiant holds his/her hands over the candles on the Altar on both sides of the Incense Burner and says:

The spread has been read.
Rune and Rede,

stone and card,
the Ancient Book we are bound to guard.
I_____, Priest(ess) and Witch close its leaves
and lay it to rest.
Let the spirit depart from its pages blest,
to come again at our behest.
Blessed be O Sacred Tarot.

The Officiant claps the hands thrice to clear the air and takes up the cards in reverse order of spreading. The cards are then put away and the candles on the Altar left to burn themselves out.

The Esbat Circle should be closed in the usual manner.

Ascent From Hades

Performed at the W.C.C. Temple in Toronto in 2000 CE

Suggested for New Moon in March. No Circle needs be cast for this rite, as it is more of a playlet for the Spring Season.

Ideally, the participants should be able to channel the God-forms they portray. However, those acting the parts could also use conventional methods of divinitory reading if not channeling the God-forms directly.

The ritual chamber is set thus:

At the North-West is a throne set for the person embodying Hades. It is dark and somber. One assistant sits on the floor beside the throne with a deck of Tarot, if the person portraying Hades is not a channeler.

At the South-East is a throne for Persephone decorated with Spring flowers. There is also an assistant with Tarot for the same reason as stated above.

The male reader personifying Hades sits on his throne with the female reader personifying Persephone sitting in his lap, both in an embrace.

One member of the Priesthood leads the Coven into the chamber, telling them:

You are summoned to the Court of Hades this night.

The Coveners take places standing around the area in a wide circle.

The Altar stands in the center of the area between the two thrones, decorated with Spring florals and burning a floral incense.

The Priest or Priestess says:

We come to celebrate Spring . . .
We mark a joyous time . . .
But our Lady is not here!

A female Covener personifying Demeter enters the chamber and stands beside the throne in the South-East. She extends her hands imploringly to the throne of Hades in the North-West.

Priest/ess:
Dame Nature bids and Great Zeus has commanded that our lady be released from cold death's embrace.
Hades! Death bringer! Transformer!
Stern one, yet of tender heart, set the world at right. Release our joy in life!

The Coven Bard begins a musical reverie or someone could sing a calling song for the Goddess. (The Celtic style *Come Lassie Come* may be appropriate.)

A female Covener as Hecate, holding a lit candle in each hand enters the ritual chamber and proceeds to move widdershins thrice around the Altar in the center of the area, symbolically descending to the Underworld to retrieve Persephone. Reaching the throne of Hades, calls Persephone to arise.

Hades and Persephone release their embrace and she stands, bidding farewell to Hades as she follows Hecate around the Altar thrice deosil, symbolically ascending from the Underworld, as the music and song continue.

Hecate delivers Persephone to the Priest/ess officiating and Demeter, who moves forward to greet her daughter. Persephone removes her dark robe and dons a robe of floral colors.

Demeter and the Priest/ess escort Persephone to her throne in the South-East and seat her there, then they both step behind her throne and stand.

The Priest/ess says:
Hail, Bright One! We rejoice you are back among us!

Hades has pulled the hood of his robe to cover his brow and sits looking dejected.

The Priest/ess says:
Coveners! New life sits among us. Go before the one who may answer your query. If your need be light go before Persephone. If matters are serious, go before Hades.

The bard plays soft music as the Coveners, one at a time, directed by the Priest/ess move to sit before Persephone or Hades.

If the Tarot is to be read, the assistant at the foot of the throne shuffles the deck and fans it out so the querent may select three cards at random, which are laid on the floor before the feet of either Persephone or Hades.

The readers personifying the Deities then read the short spread as the selected cards indicate.

Should experienced channelers be personifying the Deities, he/she speaks out the channeled impression received for that person, in which case, no assistants would be required.

After all who wish have been read, and the Priest/ess perceives the energy waning, he/she indicates to Hades, who stands up and says:

Persephone, as you are in life, I am in death. I await in darkness for your return with the Autumn. Take all and leave this place!

He turns his back on the group and stands with head bowed in sorrow as Persephone leads the group from the ritual chamber, where a party celebrating Spring may commence.

A Megalesia for the Goddess

A New Moon Esbat for April

So many times Coveners come before the Gods with personal petitions and requests for themselves and others. This is a time to honor the Goddess and offer thanks.

The Goddess is invoked and offered gifts and entertained by the Coven through its own expended energies. No questions, nor petitions are asked of Her.

This is a night for drums, music, dancing in wild abandon and feasting in honor of the Goddess.

The High Priestess, or Coven Medium, can act as vessel for the Goddess.

A roast suckling pig with breads and vegetable dishes could also be offered and some white, or rosé wine.

If the High Priestess is the medium, either the High Priest, Hand Maiden, or Practicus could be the officiant.

Two male Coveners take the part of Galli, priests of Cybele, dancing and brandishing and clashing two swords each.

The incense should be sharp, pungent, uplifting and fiery.

No Esbat Circle needs to be cast, as the dancing and wild abandon create their own atmosphere.

When all is ready, the incense is already burning in the Ritual Chamber and a throne set for the Goddess' vessel. She is escorted in and enthroned.

The officiant motions to the Summoner and he/she allows the Galli to lead the Coveners in dancing to drums and music.

The Galli give high-pitched wails and whistles brandishing and clashing their swords as they lead the Coveners around the vessel, as to raise the energy level as many times as felt necessary.

Coveners continue to dance around the vessel, until the officiant feels enough energy has been drawn in. He/she motions for silence. The music stops and the Coveners come to order around the vessel.

The officiant recites the *Orphic Hymn To The Mother of the Gods*

(The Hymns of Orpheus; Hogart; Phanes Press, 93, ISBN 0-933999-41-0, pg. 78).

The officiant then says thrice:
Great One, Goddess of all good blessings,
be with us now and accept our gifts!

He/she allows a pause for the vessel to trance and channel the Goddess.

Should the Goddess wish to speak, the Coven should be attentive. She may have messages for individuals, or words of blessing.

Should she simply manifest her presence upon the vessel, the officiant motions for the drums and music to resume, but in a more subdued manner.

The Galli have taken a position behind the vessel, where they sway back and forth, clashing their swords to the music. They are continually providing energy projected at the Goddess' manifestation. The Coven continues to dance around the Goddess and her vessel, while the officiant has the Hand Maiden, or Practicus bring the food offerings into the Ritual Chamber.

They are presented to the Goddess and she may partake, as she sees fit. Wine to drink can be offered.

The Coven sits down to also engage in the repast and libations.

Individuals and/or couples may come forward to dance or perform for the Goddess.

The Galli pick up the pace to the music, swaying, howling, clashing swords and generating energy.

The party in honor of the Goddess continues with good times and cheer.

When the energy is felt to wane, the music should grow slow and faint, allowing all to come down from the high.

The officiant then recites a license to depart:

Thank, thee, Lady, for being our guest.
Leave us now and give us rest. Blessed be our Gracious Goddess!

There should be a pause to allow the vessel to return to her normal self and then the officiant, together with the Galli, lead her from the Chamber.

The party things are cleared away and the Coven may depart.

Those acting as Galli should practice brandishing and clashing the swords in a manner to preclude any accidents during ritual.

Water Gazing as an Esbat

To develop a Coven's concentration, imagination and intuition. New Moon of May.
The Hand Maiden or Practicus could act as Officiant for this rite.

- A large clear glass chalice or bowl, 2/3 filled with water.
- One yellow and one blue candle
- A Moon Mist Oil, or a Hermes Oil.
- Burn an Incense of Jasmine and Ginger, or one of Mugwort and Mastic.

Divide the Coven into couples, gender not an issue.
It would be best if all participating had a ritual bath beforehand with salted water and oil of Camphor or Fennel. Enter the ritual area robed and anointed.
Cast the Esbat Circle in the group's usual manner.
Anoint both candles with the oil and place them to stand on either side of the chalice or bowl of water. Light them.
Set some of the incense to burn on coals.

The Officiant intones:
Luna wax, or Luna wane; Luna dark or Luna bright,
bring us mystery, or bring us light.
We seek thy gift of the second sight.
Moon which grows, or Moon which fades,
loose the visions of lingering shades,
which fleets or flashes or boldly parades,
lady, who sets the portends of the sky,
grant these visions 'ere this night doth die,
as we breathe upon the waters and attempt to scry.

Touch the rim of the chalice or bowl with the fingers of both hands as the above is chanted thrice. With the last recitation, inhale. Place both hands over the surface of the water and exhale upon its surface to make it ripple.

Scry in the water for 5-10 minutes and speak forth what is shown, whatever betide.

Each couple comes forward on opposite sides of the chalice or bowl and takes turns scrying for each other, speaking forth what is shown. When all have finished, *Close the Esbat Circle* in the group's usual manner.

Allow a discussion group for what may have been seen.

Dispose of the water out in Nature by casting it into the air to fall where it may, or into a running stream.

———————⊰❈⊱———————

Spell of the Magic Rod

Suggested for the June New Moon with a Circle casting being optional.

The Staff is the symbol of the High Priest in the Coven. It is his rod of authority in Coven affairs. A powerful tool, when properly charged, it is used to impose the collective Coven Will on persons, places and things.

An all purpose ritual for the Staff can be employed at any time by the Coven group working in unison and in one accord.

Need, not Season, or astrological times,would determine the use of this spellcraft, but best at a New Moon Esbat.

A cauldron of fresh earth is placed in the center of the Ritual Chamber, or center of the Covenstead.

Burn an Incense appropriate to the nature of the intent of the Rite itself: Rose/Lavender/Lotus for love. Mace/Nutmeg/Dill/Anise etc., for luck. Frankincense for healing. Orange/Saffron/Sandalwood for power and influence, etc., etc.

Have a red or black candle for each member of the Coven participating in the ritual. Light them all before the rite is to begin, so that the Coveners carry the candles into the Circle area with them.

The High Priest stands forth and holds his staff high, as he announces the nature of the Spell to be cast: Love, Luck, Healing, Binding etc., etc.

He then drives the staff deep into the earth in the center of the cauldron.

Each Covener steps forward in turn and touches the staff and adds his/her intention for the rite to it and his/her candle in the earth around the staff.

All joining hands, they begin to circle widdershins as they chant:

Powers of the Wizard's wand
draw in forces of the beyond.
Into this world of space and form
bringing flash of light and wind of storm.

Might and power to charge this rod
we work in the name of goddess and god.
Around the cauldron of earth and fire
set we the influence of total desire.
(each concentrates on the intention)

The chanting and the circling should grow louder and proceed faster and faster as the group circles the staff in the cauldron. When the point of exhaustion is reached, the High Priest shouts:

Peace! Be still! In the Silence of Naught. our magic doth work! It is begot!

The coven comes to order and silently sends the idea and intention of the rite to the subject or object or victim, as the case may be.

The group circles thrice deosil to unwind the knot of energy and send the idea.

The staff is taken by the High Priest and carried thrice around the person or object of the spell to bind the collective Will upon it.

How that is accomplished is up to his ability and ingenuity.

A Mind Lock has been created and set in motion.

Words of Will and Witches' Petitions

A New Moon Esbat for July

This is an out of doors rite, The High Priest acts as Officiant.

- ❧ Small fire with cauldron of boiling water.
- ❧ Holy Oil of Jasmine or Gardenia.
- ❧ small hand bell.
- ❧ copy of The Book of Esbat held flat as a tray for bell and oil.
- ❧ packet of herbs; Mugwort, Wormwood and Mullein.
- ❧ packet of gums and resins; Frankincense, Myrrh and Mastic.
- ❧ Parchment papers and pens for the Coveners petitions.

In the center of the ritual area the fire burns with the cauldron boiling water, The Staff of the High Priest rests on the ground beside it.

When it is Time for the Esbat to begin, the Coveners assemble around the fire in a circle.

The High Priest, carrying the Book of Esbat, upon which rest the hand bell and Holy Oil, herbs and resins, steps to face North across the fire.

He pours a few drops of oil into the boiling water and rings the hand bell thrice above it and says:

Holy Oil, Book and Bell summon the Will to work this spell!

He sets the Book of Esbat, with the oil and hand bell upon the ground beside the fire and takes up his staff.

The High Priest steps to the North Quarter of the Circle of Coveners. With staff in the left hand, he takes the hand of one Covener with his right. All Coveners join hands around the circle.

He leads them all in one complete circumambulation widdershins.

At the North Quarter, he thumps his staff thrice upon the ground and says:

I place the Wards of the North upon this spot!

He then leads another complete circumambulation, proceeding then past the North to the West and says:

I place the Wards of the West upon this spot!
as he thumps thrice upon the ground with the staff.

He leads them around again in one complete circumambulation, proceeding past the West to the South, where he thumps the staff thrice and says:

I place the Wards of the South upon this spot!

Leading the group another complete circumambulation, past the South to the East, he thumps the staff thrice on the ground and says:

I place the Wards of the East upon this spot!

Moving a final complete circumambulation, past the East, he bows to the North Quarter, thumps the staff thrice again and says:

The Circle is complete. This be now Witches work.

As the Coven stands in place, the High Priest moves to face North across the fire.
Setting the staff back down upon the ground, he takes up the packet of herbs.
Moving widdershins around the boiling cauldron, he sprinkles in the herbs and says:

By herb and root, by gum and oil,
let this cauldron froth and boil!

Facing North again moves widdershins around the cauldron, casting in handfulls of them, saying:

By visions in the water and steam,
enliven both desire and dream!

Facing North, again across the cauldron, he takes up the Holy Oil and moves widdershins around, pouring the remainder into the cauldron saying:

Thrice around the cauldron go,
as time and space ebb and flow.
Into it we put both wish and will,
that the world must now set to fulfill!

Music, with a lively drum beat sounds at this point, as the Coven begins to dance widdershins around the circle area.

Each Covener dances forward, around the cauldron and drops his/her written petition into the boiling water. The dance continues until the High Priest feels the energy is at its height.

He motions for the music to stop and summons all Coveners to move in close around the cauldron. Each concentrates intently on his/her private petition upon the surface of the boiling water.

Any Pagan Song of Blessing may be sung by the Coven, such as:

We give thanks for the blessing already on the way!

Then the Coven turns to face outward from the circle and points either the fingers of the strongest hand, or the Athame blade outward, as the High Priest says:

All the Elements and Gods and Goddesses bear witness to our
efforts! Send our thoughts to all corners of the Earth, as each
desire and petition seeks its own fulfillment. Blessed be!

Taking up his staff, the High Priest moves to the North Quarter of the circle and steps deosil, where he thumps the staff thrice at each Quarter, saying:

I break all Wards from this spot! Let normal time and space resume!

He rings the hand bell thrice and all Coveners may leave the circle.

The water in the cauldron should be cast upon the Earth, or into a running stream.

Do Ut Des
(I give that you may give)
Invocation of the Pagan Virtues

A High Ceremonial – A New Moon Esbat for August

- 4 Priests - each pair has a list of 10 Virtues (Performed at the W.C.C. Temple 1/14/01).
- 4 Priestesses
- 1 cauldron with several live coals
- 1 Packet of Incense; cinnamon, frankincense, myrrh and sandalwood
- 1 spoon for incense
- Small squares of parchment for Coveners to write what they will to give the Gods.
- Pens or pencils.
- 1 Large Chalice of water
- 1 Bouquet of 40 flowers
- 10 Small white candles
- 10 Small white stones
- 1 Large cauldron in center of the room containing earth
- 1 small amount of methenol

There are four stations set at the Quarters with sufficient illumination for the four pairs of Priesthood to read their lists.

Coveners are requested to write on the parchments what they will give the Gods and told to be sure to fulfill their vows as soon as possible after the rite. The parchments are carried into Circle by each Covener.

The pair of Priests at the East Quarter act as the Officiants for this rite.

The Coven is led into the Temple to any processional chant appropriate. They are arranged to stand between the four stations.

When ready, the Officiants summon the Twelve Olympians:

Priest: *Zeus, Sky Father, the best and the greatest!*

Priestess: Hera, Queen of Heaven, binder of Sacred Oaths!

Both: *Be with us now!*

Priest: *Poseidon, Earth shaker, horse breeder, rage of the sea!*

Priestess: *Athene, Maid of Wisdom, battle Queen!*

Both: *Be with us now!*

Priest: *Ares, bold one, inciter of passion!*

Priestess: *Aphrodite, beauteous one, lovers delight!*

Both: *Be with us now!*

Priest: *Apollo, shining one, truth teller!*

Priestess: *Artemis, fleet of foot, huntress of night!*

Both: *Be with us now!*

Priest: *Haiphestos, maker and shaper!*

Priestess: *Hestia, hearth fire and domestic Lady!*

Both: *Be with us now!*

Priest: *Hermes, swift messenger, market lord!*

Priestess: *Demeter, Lady of bounty and produce!*

Both: *Be with us now!*

A moment of silent contemplation to welcome the Olympians.

One of the Officiants:

We give to the Gods, that they may give to us.
As each gift is given, all will exclaim: Be thou increased!

The other Officiant:

Let us summon all the virtues taught by the Gods and given to human community! (As each Virtue is summoned and explained, a spoon of incense is placed upon the coals and *"Be thou increased"* is recited.)

Priest: *Auctoritas!*

Priestess: *Spiritual authority; the sense of one's social standing built up through experience, piety and industriousness!*

Priest: *Comitas!*

Priestess: *Humor, ease of manner, courtesy, openness and friendliness!*

Priest: *Clementia!*

Priestess: *Mercy; mildness and gentleness!*

Priest: *Dignitas!*

Priestess: *Dignity; a sense of self-worth, personal pride!*

Priest: *Firmitas!*

Priestess: *Tenacity; strength of mind, the ability to stick to a purpose!*

Priest: *Frugalitas!*

Priestess: *Frugalness; economy and simplicity of style without miserliness!*

Priest: *Gravitas!*

Priestess: *Gravity; a sense of the importance of a matter at hand, responsibility and earnestness!*

Priest: *Honestas!*

Priestess: *Respectability; the image one presents as a respectable member of society!*

Priest: *Humanitas!*

Priestess: *Humanity; refinement, civilization, learning and being cultured!*

Priest: *Industria!*

Priestess: *Industriousness; hard work!*

Then the priesthoods at the North Quarter take the lead. As each Virtue from their list of ten is summoned and explained, a drop of water from their chalice is spilt upon the bouquet of flowers at their station and the words; *"Be Thou Increased!"* are intoned.

Priest: *Pietas!*

Priestess: *Dutifulness; respect for the Gods and the Natural Order!*

Priest: *Prudentia!*

Priestess: *Prudence; foresight, wisdom and personal discretion!*

Priest: *Salubritas!*

Priestess: *Wholesomeness; health and cleanliness!*

Priest: *Severitas!*

Priestess: *Sternness; gravity and self-control!*

Priest: *Veritas!*

Priestess: *Truthfulness; honesty in dealing with others!*

Priest: *Abundantia!*

Priestess: *Abundance; plenty, the ideal of food and prosperity for all!*

Priest: *Aequitas!*

Priestess: *Equity; fair dealing by both government and among the people!*

Priest: *Bonus eventus!*

Priestess: *Good fortune, rememberance of important positive events!*

Priest: *Clementia!*

Priestess: *Clemency; mercy shown to all as persons and nations!*

Priest: *Concordia!*

Priestess: *Concord; harmony among the people and among the nations!*

The Hand Maiden, after each set of Virtues has been summoned and gifted, takes the incense cauldron from the East and places it in the larger cauldron in the center and the bouquet of watered flowers from the North and places them also in the larger cauldron.

At this point the priesthoods in the West Quarter take the lead. As each Virtues on their list is summoned and explained, one or the other, or both alternating, light one white candle and set it at their station along with the words "Be Thou Increased!"

Priest: *Felicitas!*

Priestess: *Happiness, prosperity; celebrating the best aspects of society!*

Priest: *Fides!*

Priestess: *Confidence; good faith in all commercial and government dealings!*

Priest: *Fortuna!*

Priestess: *Fortune; acknowledge positive events!*

Priest: *Genius!*

Priestess: *Acknowledgement of the Spirit of a place and its people!*

Priest: *Hilaritas!*

Priestess: *Mirth, rejoicing; to express happy times!*

Priest: *Justicia!*

Priestess: *Justice; through sensible laws and governance!*

Priest: *Laetitia!*

Priestess: *Joy, gladness, thanksgiving after the resolution of a crisis!*

Priest: *Liberalitas!*

Priestess: *Liberality; generous giving!*

Priest: *Libertas!*

Priestess: *Freedom for the arts of civilized living!*

Priest: *Nobilitas!*

Priestess: *Nobility; dignified action in the public sphere!*

The Hand Maiden takes the 10 lighted candles to the center and places them around the large cauldron.

The priesthood in the South Quarter call out and explain their list of 10 Virtues and place a white stone at their station for each one.

Priest: *Ops!*

Priestess: *Wealth; participation in the prosperity of the community!*

Priest: *Patientia!*

Priestess: *Endurance, patience; ability to weather storms; mental and physical!*

Priest: *Pax!*

Priestess: *Peace; celebrate peaceful relations between people and nations!*

Priest: *Providentia!*

Priestess: *Providence, forethought; the ability to survive trials and manifest a greater destiny!*

Priest: *Pudicita!*

Priestess: *Modesty, chastity; to avoid the appearence of moral corruptness!*

Priest: *Salus!*

Priestess: *Safety; concern for public health and welfare!*

Priest: *Securitas!*

Priestess: *Confidence and security in peace and good public order!*

Priest: *Spes!*

Priestess: *Hope for times of great difficulty!*

Priest: Uberitas!

Priestess: *Fertility in the arts of agriculture and husbandry!*

Priest: *Virtus!*

Priestess: *Courage to be a leader within the community!*

The Hand Maiden takes the 10 white stones from the South and places them within the large cauldron.

Officiants: *The hand written vows to the Gods now go into the centre!*

The Hand Maiden goes around and collects the parchments from the Coveners and casts them into the large cauldron. She stands ready with the methenol as the Offficiants say:

Officiants: *Before the High Olympians and all the virtues summoned we give thanks for these blessings and will fulfill our vows!*

The Hand Maiden sprinkles a bit of the methenol on the items in the large cauldron and then picks up one of the candles and casts it in to fire up the contents. As they blaze:

Officiiants: *Be the Gods increased! Be the virtues increased! Be we ourselves be increased! (meditation or song) we thank our ancient Gods as we depart the temple!*

The Coven files out.

The items given may vary as to food stuffs, artifacts,liquids etc., as the Priesthood may feel appropriate for the time or season.

These observances may be done whenever it is felt the community needs an infusion of Pagan Virtue.

(Author's note: Due to the amount of smoke from the incense and cauldron fire, it is suggested this rite be done out of doors.)

Ritual Invocation of Athena

Officiant - Tarostar, Medium - Lady Tamarra, High Priestess
of The Wiccan Church of Canada
Performed April 12,1992, Toronto, Ontario
At The W.C.C. Temple. Attendance: 50
Suggested as a New Moon Esbat for September

This is a rite to bless a Coven through a recitation of Pagan Virtues. The old seven virtues for time-honored ethical codes of conduct praised by the Greco-Roman writers from Ancient Times are very much lacking in our Modern World.

This is a ritual to incarnate them among the Coven.

Tarostar, of The Sacred Pentagraph Tradition, was invited to officiate as guest High Priest at the W.C.C. Sunday Circle.

This rite is offered here for those Covens and Craft Circles who may find it useful to incorporate into their own practice.

Items needed to Invest the Goddess:

- Greek or Roman Helmet
- Spear
- Round shield
- Armlets for the Goddess's wrists,
- Large Pectoral for Her Breast
- Wide belt for Her waist.

The High Priestess/Medium would wear a long Chiton, white and unbelted. Her hair should hang loose and untied.

There should be a chair set in the East of the Circle area for the Goddess's enthronement.

Below the Altar, on the floor should rest a bowl of olives, a Quaich of white wine, a Quaich of Water, a bowl of cakes or bread, a bowl of white or yellow flowers and sprigs of either olive branches, or myrtle, and an open vial or bowl of olive oil. An empty cauldron.

On the Altar should stand a small elevated image of Athena, either plaster, stone or bronze.

There should be one white and one black Altar Candle set at the North edge of the Altar flanking the image, unlit.

At the East on the Altar should rest either a Censer on a chain, or thurible with a burning coal.

The Incense is a mixture of Frankincense, Myrrh, Benzoin, Mace, Mastic, Dragons Blood Resin and Copal Gum, all of equal proportions.

To the West on the Altar should stand a silver Chalice with salted water.

A bowl of salt would rest at the North before the image of the Goddess.

To the South on the Altar should stand a small red candle, lit, and the officiant's personal Athame. Any needed notes can be set where convenient.

Quarter Candles can be lit prior to beginning to demarcate the Circle area.

The Medium must be an experienced High Priestess adept at the arts of invocation and capable of assuming the God/Goddess.

She should take a short seclusion before the rite to center and get into the right frame of mind.

As she is doing so the officiant and any assistants, such as Hand Maiden, Practicus or Summoner see to all necessities and set up.

When all is ready, at the appointed hour, the Summoner calls all Witches attending to order and leads them into the ritual chamber to stand around outside the Circle area against the walls.

The officiant and Hand Maiden stand within the center of the Circle area, ready to begin the rite.

The Summoner remains near the door to process the Lady/High Priestess/Medium into the ritual chamber and Circle area, when the Officiant indicates.

The officiant proceeds to cast the Circle in the manner of the High Priest from *The Sacred Pentagraph, Book III.*

The Hand Maiden, who has been standing within the Circle area holding her Athame and is now enclosed within the Circle along with the officiant, moves to the North-East and opens a doorway in the Circle.

She stands with Athame and challenges all Coveners to give the Coven Watchword before they enter Circle (Perfect Love and Perfect

Trust or what ever Watchword the Coven may use).

As each Covener steps to the Circle door the Hand Maiden asks:

What Gifts do you bring to this Temple?

Covener: *Perfect Love and Perfect Trust!*

As each Covener files into the Circle, he/she moves around widdershins to take a place within the Circle.

After all Coven participants have entered, the officiant says:

Let the Summoner now bring the Lady.

The Summoner leaves the ritual chamber and brings the High Priestess in procession to the doorway at the North-East of the Circle.

The officiant moves to the North-East and greets the High Priestess thus:

Extending his hands to take hers, he says:
Lady, a Temple of the Old Gods,
dedicated in perfect love and perfect trust, stands ready to
receive you. Enter and be welcome.

He leads her into the Circle, as the Summoner follows her and stands always slightly behind her in attendance.

The Hand Maiden seals the doorway and moves to assist the officiant. The High Priestess is lead to stand before the chair in the East Quarter, facing West.

The Summoner stands behind the Lady as her attendant. The Officiant and Hand Maiden stand facing the Lady across the Altar, as he begins the Invocation of the Goddess:

Maid of battle, Maid of will,
Maid of wisdom, Maid of skill,
we shall follow and fulfill.
Hail to thee, Athene! (chant by Lady Tamarra of the W.C.C.)
Bright Jove's daughter, Goddess of wisdom and war, Lady of
stratagems and wiles, be with us now and bless our bite.

As the officiant intones the invocation thrice, the High Priestess trances and assumes the Goddess. When She manifests, the officiant continues:

Lady, assume your attributes and let your virtues illumine our lives.

With the Summoner and Hand Maiden assisting, the officiant begins the investiture of the Goddess with Her attributes.

He places the helmet upon Her head and says:
This represents Rectitudo – right thinking. That which is involved in integrity and ethical social conduct.

Placing the shield upon Her arm:
This is the Jus Gentium–the Law of the Tribe; that which is best for the greatest number takes precedence over the individual. It is our shield and protection allowing the social body to continue and abide as a whole.

Handing Her the spear into her right hand he says:
This is Aequitas–the attttudes or fairness to and for all as the content of individual character does warrant.

Placing the Pectoral around Her neck, he says:
With Gravitas–responsibility, the social peace, the family, the tribe, the city and the nation are preserved.

Placing the armlets upon Her wrists, he says:
By Pietas – respect fop the ancient rites and rituals, we preserve the cosmic order and the stability of civilized society.

Fastening the belt about Her waist, he says:
With Humanitas, we see our duties to custom and act in ethical and responsible manners through all walks in life.

Stooping down, he places the myrtle or olive branches at Her feet and says:

Through all the other virtues we receive Libertas – freedom for things and not from things. the freedom to be and to do, to become and to transcend. blessed be, 0 gracious goddess.

The officiant, the Hand Maiden, the Summoner and all Coveners in Circle bow to the Goddess. The officiant says:
Lady, speak what you will. Your people await your voice.

All within the Circle sit down in place as the Goddess stands and speaks forth as She will, with what message She may have for the group.

When She has finished Her message, the Hand Maiden helps Her to sit upon the chair as the officiant places the gifts before Her: the bowl of olives, the container of oil, the quaich of wine, the quaich of water, the bowl of bread or cakes, and the flowers.

The officiant says:
Let all who wish draw near the Goddess and receive her blessing, or her admonitions; her instruction or her guidance.

He steps back and allows all who wish to come singly forward, bow before the Goddess and touch one of the items laying at Her feet.

She responds to each and reads psychically whatever message She has for him or her.

This process continues until all who wish have received a personal word from the Goddess.

Then the officiant steps before Her and says:
Lady, the hour doth wane. Lay aside your attributes and receive our gifts.

The Summoner and the Hand Maiden divest the Goddess of the items placed upon Her (Helmet, shield, spear, etc., etc.).

The officiant places the cauldron into Her lap and as he mentions each gift, he places it into the cauldron in her lap:

By the waters of life you sustain us (pours water into the cauldron).
By the wine of life you enliven us (pours wine into the cauldron).

By olive and bread you grant us bounty (puts those in the cauldron).
By oil and herb you heal us (the oil and flowers also)
The sprigs of life we return to you with grateful heart for all
your love and blessings (the sprigs of myrtle or olive are laid across
the top of the cauldron).

Then the officiant stands before the Goddess and intones the
dismissal:
We thank you, O Gracious Goddess for attending our rite. Take our
praise, our love and our blessing with you into higher realms. Hail
Athena! Hail Athena! Hail Athena! (all respond). He claps thrice
loudly to disperse the energy.

The High Priestess begins to come out of trance as the cauldron
of gifts is taken out of her lap and the Summoner conducts her from
the Circle through the doorway at the North-East, which the Hand
Maiden re-opens.

Then the officiant closes the Circle in the manner of the High Priest
from *Book III* of *The Sacred Pentagraph.*

The rite is ended and all Coveners may leave the Circle area.

(Author's note: The cauldron containing the gifts should be later
taken out of doors and some methenol or Isopropol sprinkled over it
and set alight, giving the contents to the Gods.)

THE DIONYSIA – A ROMAN FARCE

To Celebrate The Wine Harvest

Performed 9/26/04 at the W.C.C. Temple in Toronto, Ontario

Performing playlets, a Coven should have sufficient members to fill the cast with enough to also be the audience. Perhaps two or more Covens could combine efforts to stage them.

These were preformed at the W.C.C. Temple, which usually hosted upwards of about 50 or more people for the Weekly Circles.

Props:

Dramatis Personae:. . . . . . .A fan for each cast member set at their places.

Zeus . . . . .A Whoopi Cushion for Audience Member

Hera (holding her own fan) . .A Cord for Handfasting

Demeter . . . . .A Wedding/Bridal Veil

Semele . . . . .Pills and Herbs to sprinkle by Asklepios

Dionysos . . . . .Thyrsus for Dionysos

Ariadne . . . . .A Mechanical Wine Fountain set to flow

Theseus when turned on. . . .Plastic Wine Goblets

Pindar . . . . .A Couch for Theseus and Ariadne

Satyr . . . . .Chairs for Zeus, Hera, Demeter and Semele

Maenad . . . . .A Guy Fawkes Mask for Zeus

Asklepios

Audience Member

Hera's Attendant

Mise en scene: Mount Olympus looking down on the Island of Naxos.

The Summoner gives usual Charge and impresses upon the audience they are attending at the Court of Zeus and Hera.

The Hand Maiden greets the audience filing into the Temple and seats them.

On stage to begin are:

Zeus, Hera, Hera's attendant, Demeter and Pindar.

The Audience Member comes in with the rest, keeping his prop hidden. He has no fan. He takes a seat not far from Pindar.

Pindar (to audience): *Good people, let us relate the tale of dionysos and ariadne. : . . . . . .*
> *Many times we have heard the tale of Theseus and the Minotaur, of how the youths and maidens of Athens were paid as tribute to the Beast in the Labyrinth.*
> *We have heard of courageous Theseus, locked in titanic struggle with the Minotaur Beast.*
> *Of beautiful Ariadne, who provided the secret out of the Labyrinth, of how the two of them sailed off from crete and came as storm tossed lovers to the verdant Isle of Naxos . . . . .*

Enter Theseus and Ariadne. They proceed to the draped couch and sit and cuddle.

Pindar: *Little did they know this island was home to the Immortal Son of the Goddess Semele, Goddess of the Earth. Dionysos, wild rover, frenzy inducer, God of the wilds and the mountain path . . . .*

Enter Dionysos, skipping arround the area, followed by the Satyr and Maenad.

The Satyr and Maenad make lewd faces at the audience following Dionysos around.

Pindar: *Dionysos discovered the two lovers and became enamoured of Ariadne. he cast a sleeping spell of forgetfulness upon them . . . .*

Dionysos waves his Thyrsus over Theseus and Ariadne. They fall asleep upon the draped couch. He skips off stage followed by the leering Satyr and Maenad.

Pindar: *Knowing, as we do from the story, Theseus was to change the black sails on his ship to white so that his father in Athens could see his return boded success against the Minotaur.*

The Audience Member sounds his prop, the whoopi cushion. . . . .
All cast members blank and stare at him. Theseus and Ariadne sit up and stare.
The members of the cast, on stage begin to hold their noses and act disgusted.

Hera: *Wheeeeuuuuu! My fan!* (she faints in her chair).

Hera's Attendant begins to rapidly fan Hera, while holding the nose and staring disgustedly at the Audience Member. All cast members grab their fans and begin fanning toward Hera also holding their noses and glaring at the Audience Member.

Demeter: *Do something about the poor mortal's windy bowels!*

Semele: *Yes, before we have something else to deal with!*

Zeus and Hera: *Asklepios!*

Enter Asklepios, in medical gear and spilling herbs and powders.

Asklepios: *This better be important. I'm right in the middle of surgery!*

All cast members, holding their noses, point at the Audience Member.
He proceeds to stomp over to the Audience Member and dump his herbs all over the guy's head, he hands him two pills and says . . . .

Askiepios: *Take these pills tonight and sacrifice a rooster in the morning.* (he stomps out in a huff.)

Theseus and Ariadne resume their sleeping position in the bedding.

Pindar: (shocked) *Ummm, to continue . . . .*
Theseus awoke from the spell, forgetting what had happened,
and not knowing Ariadne had departed and set sail back to
Athens . . . .

Theseus gets up, stretches and departs off stage. Ariadne sleeps.

Zeus: *He left her flat. what a cad!*

Hera: *Speaking of cads, husband, how many have you loved and*
left over the eons?

Demeter and Semele giggle and hide their faces.

Zeus: *Growl, humph!* (thunder rolls, flashes.)

Hera: *Oh, stop that!* (stomping her foot) *Every time you throw a*
snit the winds get a workout!

Zeus: *Snit??? Who drove Io mad? Who persecuted Herakles? You*
throw enough snits for both of us!

Hera bats him with her fan and glares at him.

Pindar: (mortified) *I'm trying my best to relate this tale, but it ain't*
easy!!!!! (sobs, weeps).

Demeter: *Come on, let's behave and allow the poet to continue.*

Semele: *Yes, this is supposed to be about my son's wedding. I've been*
planning it for centuries.

The Olympians straighten up and get serious.

Pindar: (composes himself) *Hopefully, without further*
interruptions . . . . (he glares at the Olympians and at the
Audience Member.)

Pindar: *The frenzy God, the mountain rover, Dionysos returns to claim his prize.*

Enter Dionysos followed by Satyr and Maenad with wedding veil.

Pindar: *He awoke the sleeping Ariadn.e…and took her for his bride.*

Dionysos waves his Thyrsus over Ariadne. She awakes, stretches and gets up from the bedding.
Satyr and Maenad arrange the wedding veil upon her.

Pindar: Semele, shining Lady in the Heavens descended to Naxos and made a handfasting ....

Semele moves to stand before Dionysos and Ariadne and binds their wrists.

Pindar: *To commemorate this joyous occasion, and to lighten the hearts of mankind everywhere, Dionysos made a miracle; He created wine!*

Dionysos waves his Thyrsus over the wine fount and it starts to flow.

Pindar: *Come one, come all to celebrate this day; the glorious gift of wine!*

Dionysos, Ariadne, Satyr and Maenad process around the room leading the dance. The Bard and drummers play … "Dionysos, father of the vine" ....*
Semele and Demeter help the audience to their feet and urging them to join in the occasion.
The Satyr and Maenad set about serving the wine.
Demeter and Hera help with the wine serving to everyone. Zeus does a glamour and appears like so eone else (he dons his mask) and joins in the party.
Appropriate food/snacks to go with wine may be served.

* The words to this chant:

Dionysos, Father of the vine,
hear the dancers on the hill
singing Evoeh
for the holy wine!
Evoeh for the holy wine!
Evoeh for the holy wine!

From Lady Tamarra of the W.C.C., Toronto, Ontario

———————◆⟨⟩◆———————

JOURNEY TO THE UNDERWORLD

This is a rite of consulting the Sibyl, in the manner of Ancient Times going to the cave shrine at Cumae near the Bay of Naples. Querents would be taken into the caves and presented to the priestess and receive a word or prognostication from her.

The shrine at Cumae became very popular in Greek and Roman Times, so much so that the city itself became a perpetual Psychic fair. It flourished until Marcus Agrippa, friend of Caesar Augustus, and admiral of the Roman fleet, harvested all the forests about for shipbuilding and closed the shrine for eventually becoming notorious. Cumae was transformed into a Roman naval base and the sibyl's voice was heard no more.

This rite is suggested for the New Moon of October and was first performed 11/03/02 at the W.C.C. Temple in Toronto, Ontario. Even though it was first done in November, since the W.C.C. operates with Circles on Sundays, it should be kept in the Hallowmas Season.

There was a large group of participants for that night and they were taken in small groups from the Temple on the second floor, along the hallways and down flights of stairs to the basement, affectionately known as "The Troll Hole".

Groups doing this rite would work out the particulars with their own available facilities.

The Coven gathers in its ritual area and each Covener is given a white candle and a stalk of wheat or barley. The candles are lit just prior to setting out on the journey.

The High Priest acts as the Guide to the Underworld to take the group down, below ground to the place the High Priestess sits as the Sibyl of Cumae.

Before her rest a small cauldron burning incense of mastic and mugwort, a tray for the wheat or barley stalks and another cauldron of sand for the candles to stand.

As the guide leads the group out of the ritual chamber, he will invoke:

Dark night of the Soul, enlightenment is our goal.

Along the path to the place of descent, he says:

Down to the netherworld, the house of persephone. shades of mortal torment and blight,... shades of woe, darkness and fright, shades of anguish seeking the light, we tred your path to the realms of the dead.

Proceeding along, he says:

Step softly along the darkened ways. as the Hell Hound loudly bays. Look not back, nor to the side, lest the Night Hag upon thee ride.

A Covener acting as Cerberus at the door to the descent begins to howl and bark at the Coveners in a foreboding tone.

At the door to the descent, knocking thrice loudly on the door:

Queen of Darkness, stern Lady of Hades Abyss, we come as supplicants to your shrine, we seek the Sybil, Oracle of the Dead!

In silence the guide leads the group down to the place where the Sibyl awaits.

The Guide says to the Sibyl:

Omens for this night in time, as the deep night hours chime. Priestess of our Lady's power, we beseech thee in this hallowed hour.

The supplicants come before her and place their wheat or barley offerings in the tray and their lit candles in the recepticle of sand.

The sibyl speaks to the group, or to each, as the Goddess directs.

When the Sibyl is finished speaking, the wheat or barley stalks are set alight, as the group departs and ascends back up out of the area.

Back in the ritual chamber, the Hand Maiden and Practicus could perform the Cakes and Wine Ceremony and post-ritual refreshments can be served.

HECATE'S COURT OF DREAMS

A working by the "Dark Minions"/Coveners themselves.
Suggested for the New Moon in December.

The Coveners stage and perform the rite using the High Priestess or a Coven Woman adept at dream interpretation to channel Hecate.

First performed at the W.C.C. Temple in Toronto 11/02/01.

A ritual for dream interpretation through the power of Night.

A high seat for the vessel of the Goddess Hecate, so she is off the floor, in the center of the Temple Ritual Chamber.

The seat and Vessel face East within a semi-circle of burning black and purple candles.

There should be some white wine for the Vessel to imbibe.

Several bouquets of dark flowers with a white one in their centers set around the chamber.

An incense of Oak Moss, Patchouli and Mastic burning in a small Thurible set at the North of the Vessel.

A Hecate formula Anointing Oil set beside the Vessel.

One female Covener acts as a Hand Maiden for the Vessel to attend upon her needs as prompted.

Since this ritual is organized and performed by the Coveners themselves, the usual Coven High Priesthood participate as mere Coven members.

One is chosen to be the Officiant as "Chief Minion" and all others as "the Dark Minions".

To open the rite, all the minions/Coveners, chant in unison:

Children of the Witches ways, think of those dreams which have troubled you.
Bare them in mind and come before our Lady of the Dark, un-named Daughter of Old Night.
What dreams have made you ponder? What quandries have they posed? She, who is phosphoros will illumune them. Come to the realm of Hecate Chthonia!

All minions sit upon the floor around the high seat and the Vessel.

One of the minions takes up the incense thurible and moves widdershins outside the circle of minions, saying as he/she moves thrice around:

I make a place between the Worlds! I set this space apart!
I open the realm of my Queen of Night! Let all Lords of Light
depart, as into the Dark we go!

The Covener acting as Chief Minion steps before the Vessel and invokes:

O Chthonia; phosphoros Enodia! (thrice)
She who passes the Gates of the Realms!
She who guides the Phantasms of Night!
Lady before the Portals of Dawn!
Look kindly on us and read us those dreams found troubling.

Any song in honor of Hecate may be sung by the minions, as the Vessel assumes the Dark Goddess. One minion may chant this invocatory song:

Come, Hecate, Goddess of the Three Ways, who with your fire
breathing phantoms have been alloted dread roads and harsh
enchantments . . . .
Wings of Night bring Death and despair.
all is foul and nothing is fair.
In the Darkness we summon Your Name;
Dark Goddess, old and lame . . . .
Mormo, Gorgo, Bombo, come . . . .
Mormo, Gorgo, Bombo, come . . . .
Mormo, Gorgo, Bombo, come!

When it is felt the Goddess has arrived, the Chief Minion turns to the others and says:

Those who would have the goddess interpret a dream, hold up
your hand. Other minions will see you and present you to Hecate.

One minion takes up the anointing oil and stands beside the Vessel. He/she anoints the nape of the neck of each minion/Covener who comes forward to kneel before the Goddess and guides Hecate's hand to that spot on each person.

The minion/Covener will then tell the Lady/Vessel what dreams may be troubling. She speaks out an interpretation as directed by the Goddess.

Minions may dance and sing songs or chants for Hecate and help others go before the Lady.

Music may play softly, so as not to over-ride communion between the person and the Goddess.

When the hour or the energy wanes, the Chief Minion speaks the Dismissal:

We thank thee, Goddess of the Night!
Be propitious and keep us in thy favor.
May we summon thee again another time,
blessed be and blessed be!

One minion picks up the bouquets of flowers from their vases and moves around outside the Circle area deosil, dropping flowers as he/she goes, as the Chief Minion continues:

Let the Lords of Light return! I close the realm of my Queen of
Night, as I bring us out into the world into the Light we go!

Any after ritual festivities may begin.

Authors note: No full moon Esbats need to be done in months that there is a Sabbat.

CHANGING OF THE TIDE

November, 2nd, 2003
Toronto Temple of the W.C.C.

High Priest Officiant: Antler Crown, dark robe, sword.

High Priestess Officiant: Dark veils, cushions bearing Summer robes and jewels.

Practicus: Light colored robe, staff of a herald.

Hand Maiden: Dark veils. Assists the High Priestess during Necromancy.

Fawn: Acts as chef, serving tools for meal.

Temple Hand Maiden: Usual regalia, acts as Major Domo to seat the people and direct traffic for
the reads.

Mise en scene:

In the Southeast corner is a seat for the Dark Lord; the High Priest with a coven member as the officiant with a small table bearing Tarot Cards.

In the Northwest corner a seat for the Dark Lady; the High Priestess with a coven member as the Officiant with burning bowl for incense and empty bowl for offerings for the dead.

In the center of the Temple a table containing the feast; beef, vegetables, breads, etc., and serving essentials.

Summoner's Charge:
At this season of Samhain the Dark Lord assumes rule.
The Lady of Light departs into the Underworld leaving us to His
cold embrace. The Dark Lord invites you to feast.
Are you worthy of His bounty?.
Have you reaped what you have sown?

The Summoner leads the people into the Temple. The Bard may play a dirge as processional music.

The temple Hand Maiden seats the people around the feast table, keeping a space clear before both the seat for the Dark Lord and the seat for the Dark Lady.

The Practicus, the Hand Maiden, and a coven member acting as the fawn stand by the feast table. The Dark Lord and Dark Lady stand by their respective seats.

The Temple Hand Maiden, once having seated the people, stands by the Summoner, attentive to any needs the people may have.

The Practicus:
Beloved ones, the time of the Lord of Death has come
upon us again. The wheel of life turns around, the tides reverse
and the cycles continuously change.
On this darksome night His power waxes, while that of the Lady
wanes. To this end we prepare to relinquish the crown and draw
deep within that we may replenish the force of love and light for
times to come. So be it.

The Practicus proceeds to cast the Circle all around the assembled people, widdershins, saying:

I conjure thee, O Circle of Power that thou be foremost a boundary
between the world of mortals and the realms of the Mighty Ones.
blessed be that which is purified by ritual summoning of Earth,
water, fire and air.

The Practicus repeats the foregoing at the four Quarters around the assembled people.

Back in place, he speaks to the Dark Lord:

We fear thee, Lord, for one of thy faces is Death yet, Thou offerest
needed rest and repast. The dying fires of the midsummer sun
extinguish in Thy icy breath.
(Dark Lord only nods in silence.)
Turn, turn, the wheel doth turn
and on it souls like candles burn . . . .
one swiftly, one slowly, one flickers out . . . .
yet turning, yet burning and so round about.

Practicus cont. turning to face the Dark Lady;

Before the season is upon us, the Lady must grant her charge.

The Hand Maiden goes to the Dark Lady and takes the cushion bearing the Summer regalia and proceeds to lay them near the seat of the Dark Lord in his corner and returns to stand beside the Dark Lady.

High Priestess/Dark Lady:
We place the summer at your feet.
All hail, O Horned One! Ride the wind and in the wild chase hunt the hind. As by the fire we wait the blast and harken 'til the hunt is passed.
O ye, who seek the death of man, pray, spare as many as you can, by sparing with the wind that chills and brings with it the winter ills. Be frugal with the snow and rain that we might fill the earth again and dig the ground and turn the sod.
Be kind to us, O dreaded God!

The High Priestess/Dark Lady seats herself upon her chair with the Hand Maiden on the floor beside her, in attendance.

Practicus:
Lord of Winter and misrule, Thy turn is at hand . . . .we commend ourselves to thy care.
Pray, favor thy Wiccan children.
If it be Thy just decision to take some from among us, this cold and harsh season, we ask that those souls be returned to earth in the fullness of time, to be reborn into a true Wiccan family, among a loving Coven of the Ancient Faith.
We have always been a joyous people, with love in our hearts for all creation for as surely as the sun returns to illuminate each day, and one season follows upon another . . . .
we know that all must rest to be renewed. The sleep Thou givest is but a short watch in the night.

The High Priest/Dark Lord seats himself as the Practicus moves to sit beside his seat and assist with the Tarot reads.

The Hand Maiden stands to face the High Priestess/Dark Lady and says:

Thou art my lamp, O Gracious Mother. The Lady will lighten our darkness. Behold, the night falleth and darkness covers the Earth, but Thy candle, dear Lady, shineth upon my heart; and by Thy light we tread through the darkness.
Yea, the blackness is no fetter with thee.
The night is as clear as the day.
The darkness and the light to thee are as one. Bleseed be.

The Hand Maiden continues, turning to the people:
Good brothers and sisters of the Craft, the Lord and Lady bid you to feast. Partake of the bounty and be well.
Those who would commune with the departed, this eve, take of the raw foods and go to the Lady and deposit that offering.
Those who would seek a word for the season ahead, go to the Lord and draw of the cards.

She returns to sit by the Lady and assist as needed.

The Bard may begin a soft musical interlude.

The Temple Hand Maiden moves to assist the Fawn at the serving table and help direct the traffic flow in the circle.

The Fawn begins to serve up the repast.

At the Lord's place, the Practicus will shuffle the cards for each querent and allow them to draw three cards, which they place before the Lord on the small table.

He reads as they fall.

At the Lady's place, supplicants place the raw meat in the offering bowl and take a small candle, which is lit and placed in a cauldron for the spirit they would call through the Lady.

The feast and reads continue, until the time wanes.

Both the Practicus and Hand Maiden proceed to close the Circle thus:

He moves deosil, she moves widdershins from the North, passing each other in the South and back to the North, saying:

It is done, the power has been released. The Sabbat work is over. Blessed be.

The feast may continue.

January Full Moon Ritual

HECATE'S COURT OF DREAMS

A ritual for dream interpretation through the Power of Night.

A high seat for the Vessel of Hecate, so she is off the floor, in the centre of the Temple.

The seat and Vessel facing East within a semi-circle of black and purple candles.

White wine for the vessel to imbibe.

Several bouquets of dark flowers with a white one in their centres. Incense of Oak Moss, Patchouli and Mastic, burning in a small cauldron to the North of the Vessel.

A Hecate formula anointing oil.

Hand Maiden to attend upon Vessel's needs as prompted.

The Summoner assembles the Coven and gives any instructions as necessary.

Dark Minions are coven members: (howls, cackles, shrieks)—enter they and say to the Coven, in unison, as a Greek Chorus:

Children of the Witches ways, think of those dreams which have troubled you. – Bear them in mind and come before our Lady of the Dark; unnamed daughter of Old Night.
What dreams have made you ponder? What quandries have they posed? She, who is phosphoros, will illumine them.
Come to the realm of Hecate Chthonia!

(Howls, cackles, shrieks) they lead the Coveners into the Temple and arrange them to sit in a circle around the high seat and the Vessel.

One of the minions takes up the incense and moves widdershins, outside the circle of Coveners, saying, as he/she moves thrice around:

I make a place between the worlds! I set this space apart! I open the realm of my Queen of Night! Let all Lords of Light depart. As into the Dark we go!

The incense is set back in place and more added as needed.

The Chief Minion steps before the Vessel and invokes:

O Chthonia; Phosphoros Enodia (repeat thrice).
She who passes the gates of the realms!
She who guides the Phantasms of Night!
Lady before the Portals of Dawn!
Look kindly upon us and tell us those dreams found troubling.

Any song in honor of Hecate may be sung by the minions, as the Vessel assumes the Dark Goddess. One Minion may sing the Invocatory Song:

Wings of Night bring death and despair
all is foul and nothing is fair
in the darkness we summon Your Name;
Dark Goddess, old and lame
Mormo, Gorgo, Bombo, come
Mormo, Gorgo, Bombo, come
Mormo, Gorgo, Bombo, come

(The above set to music and sung by a Dark Minion after the Chief Minion invokes the Goddess upon the Vessel.)

When it is felt the Goddess has arrived, the Chief Minion turns to the Coveners and says:

Those who would have the Goddess interpret a dream hold up
your hand. The Dark Minions from Hades will see you and
present you to Hecate.

One Minion takes the anointing oil and stands beside the Vessel. He/she anoints the nape of the neck of each Covener who comes forward and guides Hecate's hand to that spot on the Covener.

The Covener will tell the Lady what troubles him/her in dreams. She speaks an interpretation as the Goddess directs.

Minions dance and chant a Hecate Song, lowly in tone and help each Covener to stand up and be presented in turn. Music may sound, but not to over-ride the communion between Covener and Goddess.

When the hour wanes, the Chief Minion speaks the dismissal:

We thank thee, Goddess of the Night.
Be propitious and keep us in Thy favour.
May we summon Thee again some other time.
Blessed be and blessed be.

One minion takes up the bouquets of flowers from their vases and moves outside the circle of Coveners and steps deosil all around, dropping flowers as she/he goes, saying:

Let the Lords of Light return! I close the realm of my Queen of Night, as I bring us out into the world into the Light we go!

Lights in the Temple go on. Coveners file out.

———————⟡———————

FULL MOON OF MAY:
THE OLD WHITMAST TIDE
THE MAY WINE MOON RITUAL

This Esbat rite is a communion with Deity by the Coven and used to raise psychic consciousness to an at-one-ment with God/Goddess. It does not work any heavy magic, but does open the psychic channels to the Old Gods and places one in their mystic embrace.

The items needed for this ritual are quite simple and easy to set up and accomplish.

The Altar should be dressed in white and be set with May-time Spring flowers. Thirteen white candles should be burning in a row on the Altar.

Upon it will rest a large plate containing 13 slices of the darkest and richest Rye Bread available.

There should also be 13 chalices of the headiest red wine money can buy (twelve for the Coven, one for the Gods).

All participants are to have fasted for 24 hours prior to the ceremony. To get the full benefit from this rite, the above stipulation is essential. The incense used in this ritual should be mercurial, such as benzoin or mastic with a bit of Basil and Mace or ground nutmeg blended in.

That would also help in opening the psychic channels.

It would be best to dispence with the usual method of casting the Circle for this Esbat and just assemble the Coven around the area of the Altar. The twelve participants, forming a closed circle by holding hands around the Altar, would make the proper psychic link.

The thirteen white candles are lit and the incense set to fill the ritual chamber.

The High Priest and High Priestess stand facing North across the Altar, as the Practicus and Hand Maiden join hands with the rest of the Coven and enclose them within.

The High Priest places his hands in blessing over the chalices of wine, as the High Priestess does the same for the bread.

Together they pray:

Hear us,. God and Goddess of our Ancient Faith. Let Thy power
and blessing pour forth upon this Coven and at this Wiccan Altar.
Reach out to us, as we reach out to Thee.
Thou art God and Goddess; creation's Supreme Being. Thou art
God, thou art mankind.
Be what Thou wilt as one.
God and Goddess, bless these elements of wine and rye that
through them we may come closer and experience Thy love and
light. Blessed be.

The High Priestess passes the plate of the rye around the circle
widdershins, each person taking a slice.

The plate with the one remaining slice of rye is set back upon the
altar to stand for the Goddess.

The High Priest passes each a chalice of wine around the circle area
widdershins so each person takes one.

The last, or thirteenth chalice of wine remains upon the Altar to be
for the God.

Both officiants (High Priest and High Priestess) say together:

Come all Coveners and partake of this Whitmastide blessing. as
the spirit of the Gods reaches out to bless the world at this full
moon, seek ye all in inward communion to be and become as one
with them.

All Coveners eat the rye and sip the wine until they are constuned.
The chalices are replaced upon the Altar.

Then the whole Coven recites this Litany of the Gods:

Lady of this full moon night,
bring thy consort; the God of Light. God of Life, our Lord
Supreme, bring Thy Lady; Heaven's Queen.
We lift our spirits high to Thee,
from field and dell and shore of the sea. Do not linger so far away,
come to this circle and with us stay.
Lift us into Thy power and might, be here on this Esbat night.
Thy children call and cry to Thee. To Thy comfort we shall flee.
Gods of our most Ancient Faith and Way mingle and conjoin and

with us play. We accept Thy Will into our minds. Witchery's way us to thee binds.

After the recitation, the High Priest and High Priestess step into the circle of Coveners, joining hands with them and begin to lead a circle dance widdershins taking up this chant, to which all join in, as the circle dance proceeds faster and faster:

Rye and wine
make this night fine.
We seek our Gods by dance and tune. We read their Will by rede and rune.
They speak in silence and teach by love, bringing inspiration from above.
Rye and wine and wine and rye,
by them let our spirits ply.
Let the power of fast and prayer
the veils of existence rip and tear.
By the ergot, by the wine, by the chant and by the dance,
our heightened minds we do enhance. By the light of Lady and Lord, let channels open, as we implored.
Come, O Full Moon, to the May Wine Feast. Let all vex and stripe be ceased.
Come O Full Moon to this Esbat rite, and bathe us in thy sacred light.

The High priesthood keep the circle moving and the chanting going until it is felt enough energy has been raised and until the wine and ergot begin to affect the empty stomachs of the Coveners.

(The psychic will open)

Then they bring the circle to order and all sit down around the Altar and go into a meditative silence, each communing with God/Goddess in the privacy of inner space.

As the silence proceeds, let each commune and hold what thoughts impign upon him/her and remember them.

After a good 15 minutes of meditation, the High Priestess can then begin to ask each person what he/she may have experienced.

Allow each Covener who wills to share his/her thoughts with the others. However, do not force one to divulge what may be felt to be a personal or a private message from the God/Goddess.

When the power begins to drain off and wane the High Priest should stand up and say:

Thank thee Lady of the May Wine Moon.
We have seen and heard Thy Witchy rune.
Return to Thy heaven's orb in flight.
We bless Thee on this Esbat night.

The High Priestess then claps the hands thirteen times to dispell the vibration and return normal time and space.

The Altar arrangement may be cleared away and the results of the rite properly recorded.

Proceed into a short supper or refreshment to off set the wine and ergot on empty stomachs.

Full Moon of July
Council of Elders

The full Coven does not meet this night. Present are members of the High Priesthood from all Covens which can trace their origin to the work of those in the district, or Covendom, who are the Elders, and those of the V⁰ in the Covendom; a Magister Sacrorum, a Queen Mother and a Philosophus and Oracle, should there be any in the district.

The members of the High Priesthood are IV⁰ and junior members of the Council. There may be as many as the Elders have elevated to the High Priesthood over the years.

There may also be as many of the V⁰ as there are in the district.

With time, the Council will grow to a full compliment of persons.

However, the Council meets at one Covenstead or another, as it sees fit, for ideally, it should meet at different Covensteads on different years.

That way each Covenstead receives the honor of hosting a Council. For the opening ritual to follow, the host Covenstead should perform the rite.

All other members of High Priesthoods attend, but sit around the outer area and allow the hosting High Priest and High Priestess to celebrate the ritual.

The Elders take their seats to the sides against the opposite walls, as per the diagram that follows.

Should there be more than one Elder of the same level, he/she would allow the Elder more closely associated with the hosting Coven to have the seat of honor for the ritual.

On the Altar at the far end of the Ritual Chamber, sits two three-branched candlesticks bearing candles of the kundalini colors. Also will rest there the agenda and notes for things to be considered by the Council.

At the opposite end will be a small table bearing the host Coven's Sacred Flame and two lit white candles, which the High Priestess has lit previous to the beginning of the Council.

The hosting High Priesthood stand beside the small table as the Elders take their places.

The hosting High Priesthood begins the ritual by taking up each one of the two lit white candles from the small table.

The High Priestess says:

We of the Coven of _____ welcome our Lord and Lady Elders and all visiting High Priesthood. Blessed be!

The High Priest then says:

May the blessings of the Old Gods guide the deliberations of this council.

They then move across each other's path to the opposite wall and stand before the seats of the elders. The High Priest before the Philosophus, Magister and Oracle. The High Priestess before the Queen Mother and the two empty seats, which the hosting High Priesthood, themselves., will take later.

They lift up the candles they hold before the elders and say:

In the light of the Sacred Flame, by the power of the Ancient Gods, we call the spirit of justice and equinimity to guide this council in all its serious business. Blessed be!

Then they proceed to the opposite sides of the Altar, crossing each other's path once again.

At the opposite corners of the Altar they light the candles in the two triple-branched candlesticks, from the outside inward, with these words:

May tie fires of the Divine Light and Sacred Energy mix and mingle in this council to give all persons participating true and uplifting divine inspiration. Let all opinions be heard and all facets of questions be duly and fairly expressed. May the good God and gracious Goddess be with us in this hour. Blessed be!

Snuffing out their candles, they set them on the corners of the Altar

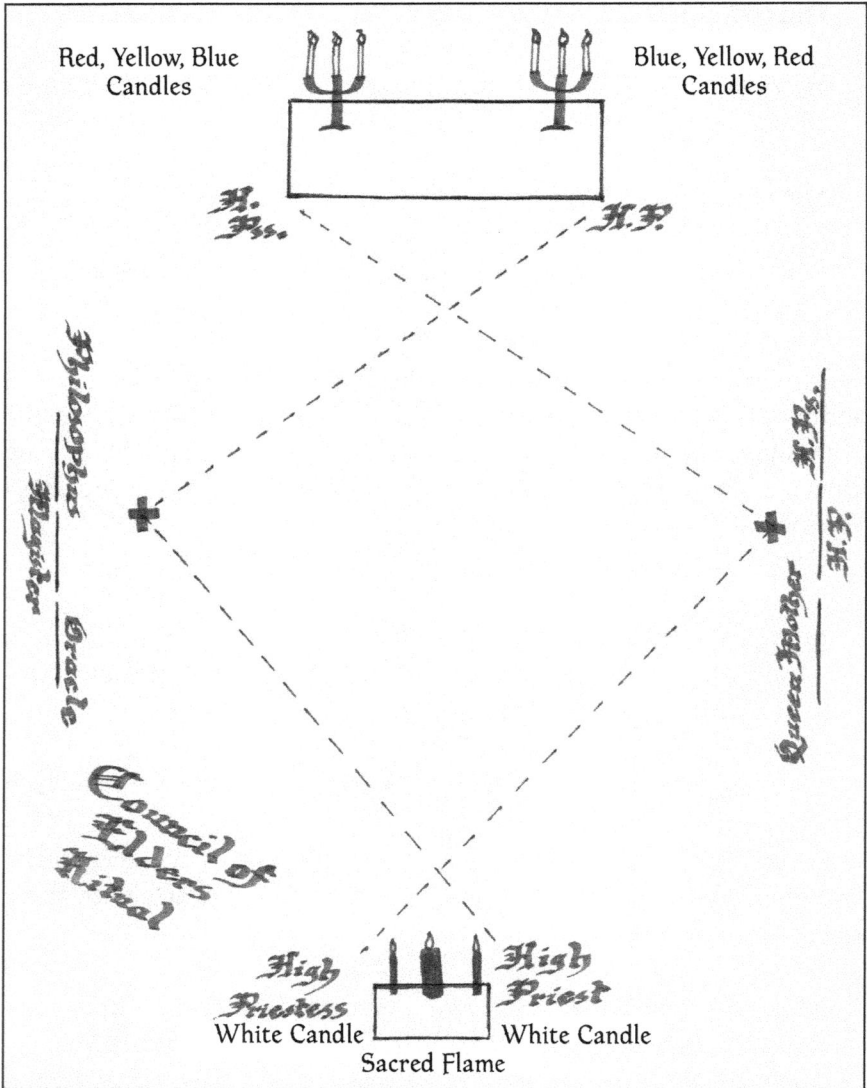

Red, Yellow, Blue Candles

Blue, Yellow, Red Candles

H. Fs.

H. P.

Philosophus

Magister

Oracle

H. Fs.

H. P.

Queen Mother

Council of Elders Ritual

High Priestess

High Priest

White Candle

White Candle

Sacred Flame

and both walk to their seats beside the queen Mother.

Then the Scribe of the Council of Elders, either the Magister or Queen Mother, stands forth and says:

I, Magister Sacrorum/Queen mother V°, and scribe of the Council of Elders, declare the proceedings of this council for the year ____ in the Covendom of _____ now open. Blessed be!

From this point the Elders and High Priesthood deliberate as is the custom for the Covendom.

(See *Books I, II, & III* for matters done at a Council of Elders).

After the Council meeting the candles on the Altar are snuffed out in reversed order of lighting.

THE CORNUCOPIA

Spells, spellcasting, divination and the Arts of
Low Magic along with the teaching guides for the
true method of training in the Craft.

The Sacred Pentagraph

BOOK V

THE CORNUCOPIA

INTRODUCTION

In keeping with the other tomes of *The Sacred Pentagraph*, this volume contains the teaching outline for the High Priesthood to use in bringing persons up to the level of becoming a First Degree.

The *Book of the Wise I* is for the Pre-Initiate to prepare for the taking of the Neophyte level Initiation.

Book of the Wise II is the basic course outline from which the High Priesthood may draw their lectures and reading assignments. Those lessons prepare one to take the Probationer level.

Book of the Wise III is the continuing study for the Probationer to prepare one to take the First Degree Initiation, Becoming a Craftsman First Degree.

Those three levels of Initiation bring one into full status as a Witch. As *The Book of Beginnings, Book II of The Sacred Pentagraph* states, any further advancement in the Craft is optional from that point.

The next section of this tome gives various suggestions for Spellcraft and the Magical Arts within the Craft. Spells and Talismans are offered and suggested for the further advancement in the Craft for those wishing to take the Second Degree level of Initiation, becoming Artisan.

However, that level is sought on one's own without any training or classes held by the High Priesthood.

Responsibility, integrity and self discipline are laid upon the individual him/her self in studying the Ars Magica.

The system of *The Sacred Pentagraph* is difficult and demanding, but it does produce the very best in the line of Students on the road of Adepthood in the Occult Arts and Psychic Sciences.

The ideal is always held up to the Student to try and embody. No form of compromise can and will be tolerated in study and application. To allow otherwise would do the Student and the Craft dishonor.

If you seek an easy way and a less involved method, this system is not recommended. It can only be mastered from the beginning and by working it through to the end. That may not be possible in one life time.

However, if the Perfecting of being is what you seek in The Old Religion, this method can be numbered among the best.

Many will try. Most will fail. But the ideal will still stand. Some will persevere to the end. In that way the Ancient Wisdom Tradition will not vanish from the face of the Earth.

The Book of The Wise 1
The Precepts of Cosmic Order

Knowledge and mastery of which lead to
the grade of Neophyte.

Tarostar V⁰
Magister Sacrorum
Circle of Starmeadow
Ancient Order of Bell Book and Candle, Las Vegas, Nevada.
1986 ce

These are the Redes and Rules offered to the Pre-Initiate in the Why of the Wise, in order that he/she may align his/her spiritual nature toward the life of balance and harmony as taught by the Craft:

I. It is an eternal Law of the Cosmos that there be no effect without a cause. The seed will produce a harvest by the Law of "Like Produces Like".

II. It is the law of Mind that "As a man thinketh—so is he.". Life is formed from the inside out. Thoughts are the transformations one releases in life.

III. It is an eternal Law of the Cosmos that to live is to function. Therefore, work and effort are the result of function. That which does not function must die..

IV. It is the Law of Mind that "Belief is Power." The act of believing is the force that leads to accomplishment.

V. It is the Law of Mind that mental attitude is more important than mental capacity. One can only make others feel that which one demonstrates by attitudes.

VI. It is an eternal Law of the Cosmos that only the fit survive. Therefore, life is a great battle.

VII. It is an eternal Law of the Cosmos that growth and maturity are the goals of all life.

Maturity of body should lead to maturity of spirit. When things stop growing, they begin to die . . . .

VIII. It is an eternal Law of the Cosmos that life is to learn experience. One must learn to live in order to handle any and all things life may bring.

IX. It is the Law of Mind that misfortune is born of the inability to make proper choices. To Man is given the power to choose. Let Him, therefore, choose well, for most of life depends thereon.

X. It is the eternal law of the Cosmos that there is only one supreme and absolute power as the source of all Life. The duality of Nature (the Gods) is but a name for the effect of Source.

XI. It is a Law of Mind that to improve the external world, one must first improve the internal person. One should always attempt self-discovery and adhere to the Dictum: "Man, Know Thyself". For such is the sum of all wisdom.

XII. It is a Law of Mind that one must make contact with the full environment in order to commence living. Therefore, one must distinguish living from mere existing.

XIII. It is a Law of Mind that material things must be kept in proper perspective. They are only tools, or a means to an end. Not the and in itself.

XIV. It is an eternal Law of the Cosmos that one must live life before one can understand it. Not all things in life may be proven, nor may all things be defined. Certain things have their mysteries.

XV. It is an eternal Law of the Cosmos that that which is natural is also simple and of abiding greatness. One must acquire naturalness in all circumstances and forego false impressions. The Wise will ever seek to simplify their lives and cut away complexities.

XVI. It is an eternal law of the Cosmos that all things must flow with life. One must adapt to conditions and not oppose what cannot be changed, but change the things which can be.

XVII. It is a Law of Mind that Mankind is designed for action. Not what one knows, but what one does is that which counts. If one allows the world to go by - it will.

XVIII. It is an eternal Law of the Cosmos that moderation within order is the key to satisfaction in life. One must stay in balance and harmony with one's concept of the Creator, the Gods or Source.

XIX. It is an eternal Law of the Cosmos that that which is used will increase and that which is abused or misused will decrease.

Therefore, one must use all things correctly. The right use of all faculties will increase their. effectiveness.

XX. It is an eternal Law of the Cosmos that change is the only thing that abides. The secret of success is to adapt to things as they change. What becomes an obstruction is flushed away.

XXI. It is a Law of Mind that Man is a creature of habit. Success is a habit as well as failure. What one habitually does is the real person.

XXII. It is an eternal Law of the Cosmos that adversity exists only to be striven beyond. The more opposition one faces, the better are the chances for moving ahead. Only by accepting defeat as a reality is one ever truly defeated.

XXIII. It is an eternal Law of the Cosmos that nothing ever moves without a mover. The Law of Inertia states anything in a state of being will continue in that state whether resting or moving. One must, therefore, use that law to advantage rather than disadvantage.

XXIV. It is a Law of Mind that there is a Wolf in Man. Human nature must be tamed to serve rather then allowed to rule.

XXV. It is a Law of Mind that Man is designed for success. In order to obtain success one mast do more for the world than the world does for one. Then only is success obtained on the physical, mental and spiritual planes.

XXVI. It is a Law of Mind that happiness is created not by how much one has, but by how much one enjoys that which one has. Happiness is joy, which is spiritual prosperity.

XXVII. It is a Law of Mind that responsibility educates and helps to make life better. Man is born into this world to perform His duty. That duty is meeting the day's demands responsibly.

XXVIII. It is an eternal law of the Cosmos that Time limits Man's existence. One should only live one day at a time. The cost of anything is the amount of time spent obtaining it.

XXIX. It is a Law of Mind that one must be ever aware of one's own limitations. Each one's resources and privileges are limited only by oneself.

XXX. It is an eternal Law of the Cosmos that creativity is eternal. Each individual has creative ability. One's Imagination is more valuable than one's knowledge.

XXXI. It is an eternal. Law of the Cosmos that vitality wasted imposes severe consequences. Food and fresh air preserve the body, but right thinking preserves the mind. One must not waste energy on unnecessary fears and worries.

XXXII. It is a Law of Mind that one should ever cultivate the best within oneself. One must ever seek to become more noble and find ones own true worth.

XXXIII. It is an eternal Law of the Cosmos that noble parents have noble children. Heredity and environment make Man what He is..

XXXIV. It is an eternal Law of the Cosmos that to give is to get. One best serves oneself who looks for privileges of service. The universe pays each one according to what is given out.

XXXV. It is an eternal law of the Cosmos that the Law of Moral Worth produces penalties for unmoral conduct and rewards for moral action. Behavior is the mirror which shows one's own true image..

XXXVI. It is an eternal Law of the Cosmos that all needs are met. One must truly distinguish between needs and wants. Wants do not always make for happiness.

XXXVII. It is a Law of Mind that one makes or unmakes oneself.Self-discipline is the tool with which success is forged.

XXXVIII. It is an eternal Law of the Cosmos that prayer brings communion with the Infinite. It is the belief one exercises in the heart that brings results.

XXXIX. It is an eternal Law of the Cosmos that all things show gender.. There must be a union of the heart in order for persons to unite. Otherwise the Law of Sexual Attraction operates destructively.

XL. It is a Law of Mind that life is made or ruined by one's habitual thinking. Proper adjustment to life avoids mental illness.

XLI. It is an eternal Law of the Cosmos that Love cements the universe. There are two kinds of Love: "Agape", that which builds up, and "Eros", that which tears down. One must always strive for the constructive aspect of Love. Love does not explain the Gods, it reveals them.

XLII.. It is a Law of Mind that the sum of experience is stored in memory. Communion with yesterday will enrich today.

XLIII. It is an eternal Law of the Cosmos that all actions and attitudes effect others. "No man is an island unto himself."

XLIV. It is an eternal Law of the Cosmos that Spirit is the power in Man. The greatest contribution one can make is to live at one's spiritual best.

XLV. It is an eternal Law of the Cosmos that Freedom is the natural state of all life. Freedom does not mean license or avoidance of responsibility. One needs freedom for something rather than freedom from things.

XLVI. It is an eternal Law of the Cosmos that all Nature ages. To live is to function and each hour should be made rich with value and beauty. Let not the body die because it is infested with a dying mind. Age should be the most beautiful time of life.

XLVII. It is an eternal Law of the Cosmos that all endings are new beginnings. Life's end is its beginning. All wisdom teaches that nothing disappears without a trace. Nature knows not extinction, only transformation. To die is to gain.*

Such are the Witch's Redes for these days of wrath and anguish. Let them guide the Children of the Good God and the Gracious Goddess into the Future.

Blessed Be!

Tarostar
7/2/82 Luna waxeth in Sagittarius

* Author's Note: In her many visits to the Bell Book & Candle Shop in Las Vegas, NV in the late 1970's, Sybil Leek gave Lady Charmaine a copy of a book called *The Supreme Philosophy of Man.* It was her suggestion perhaps the ideals expressed therein could find a place in the Sacred Pentagraph system.

It was thought appropriate to present those ideals as these Precepts.

THE BOOK OF THE WISE II

OF THE MAGICAL UNIVERSE AND THE ANCIENT GODS

Teaching plan for the high priesthood
Lessons for the Neophyte in the Way of the Wise
(Leading to the grade of Probationer)

Tarostar V[0]
Magister Sacrorum
Circle of Starmeadow
Ancient Order of Bell Book and Candle, Las Vegas, Nevada.

As Elders in the Craft, it is not Our intention to impose dogmatic or fast rules concerning the lessons given to Neophytes by established Covens and presently active members of the High Priesthood.

However, certain standards of intellectual capacity and aspects of knowledge should be mastered and displayed by any candidate for advancement in the grades of the Craft in the Way of the Wise.

Levels of Initiation must, first of all, be earned. Mastery of Craft Lore should be taught to facilitate such advancement.

These lessons for the Neophyte are given as suggestions to help augment the classes and information which the High Priesthood should require of anyone seeking to advance into the grade of Probationer.

They are designed to cover one full year of monthly assignments and personal application applied in conjunction with weekly lectures on these subjects given at the discretion of the High Priesthood and/or Artisans II Degree acting as teachers under the direction of the High Priesthood.

The books for reading and research are suggested by the Elders as being the best[1] available which contain the elementary knowledge required for the Neophyte preparing to advance in the Craft.

---

1 - Best available at the time of writing this manuscript. Since then, more recent books and texts have become available on the market, which those teaching the Craft may apply.

As soon as a person has been initiated as a Neophyte at the Vernal Equinox, he or she must than begin the study for the next stage in the initiatory levels of the Craft.

The Neophyte may research these books in a Public Library, the Coven Library, or purchase them for personal use when available.

The first Month after the Neophyte's Initiation should be devoted to learning about and understanding the Magical Universe.

At the weekly classes there should be lectures concerning the high points of the subject and discussions of the various viewpoints of the authors herein suggested:

Theories of Cosmogenesis: Magic, an Occult Primer; David Conway; E.P. Dutton & Co.; New York; pg. 19-60.

Occult Powers in Nature and in Man; Geoffrey Hodson; The Theosophical Publishing House; pg. 3-87.

The Tree of Life: A Study in Magic; Israel Regardie; Samuel Wiser; New York; pg. 23-101.

A written test on the Theories of Cosmogenesis should be given at the end of the Month.

The second Month should be given over to the study of the nature of the Gods of the Craft.

The Neophyte is taught that all the Gods of Antiquity are but various aspects of the Primordial All-Father and that all the Goddesses of earlier epochs are but the different faces of the Ancient Earth Mother.

Lectures on the ancient Mythologies should be given and readings assigned to augment:

Mytholgy; Edith Hamilton; Mentor Books.

Gods and Myths of Northern Europe; H.R. Ellis Davidson; Penguin Books.

Witches: Investigating an Ancient Religion; T.C. Lethbridge; Citadel Press.

Plus, any of the good books on the Ancient Egyptian Religion, of which there are too many to list, and the old standard by Margaret Murray, *The God of the Witches.*

At the end of the Month a written test should be given to cover general knowledge of Mythology.

The third Month should be devoted to the History of the Craft from earliest times through "The Burning Time" up to the repeal of the Witchcraft Laws. Lectures in Craft History should be supplemented with readings from:

Witchcraft, the Old Religion; L.L. Martello; University Books Inc.
An ABC of Witchcraft Past and Present; Doreen Valiente; St. Martins.
The Secrets of Ancient Witchcraft; Crowther and Crowther;
    University Books.

A written test should be given covering a general knowledge of Craft early History.

The fourth Month should continue with teaching the History of the Craft since the repeal of the Witchcraft Laws (1736 and 1951).

There should be lectures on the modern Revival of the Craft and contain information about the individuals who have contributed to this revival. Several assignments for reading should be given from such books as:

Diary of a Witch; Sybil Leek; Mentor Books (plus any of her other books on the Craft).

Books about Alex Sanders:
King of the Witches; J. Johns; Coward McCann; N.Y.
What Witches Do; Stewart Farrar; Coward McCann; N.Y.

Books by Raymond Buckland:
Witchcraft: Ancient and Modern; H.C. Publishers; N.Y.
Witchcraft From the Inside; Llewellyn Publications.

Books by the Crowthers:
The Witches Speak; Weiser; N.Y.
Witchblood; L.C. Publishers; N.Y.

Also such books as:
The Anatomy of Witchcraft; Peter Haining; Taplnger; N Y.

Witchcraft, the Sixth Sense; Justine Glass; Wilshire Book Co. (seems to be a rehash of Gerald Gardner's *Meaning of Witchcraft*).
The Grimoir of Lady Sheba; Llewellyn Publications.
Witch; Lady Sheba; Llewelyn Publications.

A written test should be given concerning general knowledge of the works of the modern writers on the Craft, Gardner to the present.

The fifth Month should be devoted to the comparative study of the various Traditions within the Craft.

Lectures should explain the differences and the basic similarities between the Gardnerian, Alexandrian, Celtic, Welsh, Sicilian, etc., groups within the Craft.

One is advised also not to neglect the sister Faiths to the Craft such as the Macumba, the Santeria and the Voodoo. They should also be taught and researched.

The reading assignments are recommended from such works as:

Drawing Down the Moon; Margot Adler; Viking Press.
The Spiral Dance; Starhawk.
The Tree: The Complete Book of Saxon Witchcraft; R. Buckland, Weiser N.Y.
Witchcraft Today; Gerald B. Gardner; Citadel Press.
Mastering Witchcraft; Paul Huson; G.P. Putnam's Sons; N.Y.

(Plus any of the aforementioned books from the third and fourth Month's lessons, and any of the recent publications put out by Covens as newsletters and the magazines such as old copies of *Gnostica* and *Green Egg*).

Macumba: The Teachings of Maria Jose; Serge Bramly; Avon Publishers..
Macumba; A. J. Langguth; Harper and Row.
Santeria; Gonzales-Wippler; Anchor Books.
Romany Magic; Charles Bowness; Weiser N.Y.
Gypsy Demons and Divinities; Charles Bowness; Weiser N.Y.
Gypsy Sorcery and Fortune Telling; C.G. Leland; University Books.
Divine Horsemen: The Voodoo Gods of Haiti; Maya Deren; Delta.
The Complete Book of Voodoo; Robert W. Pelton; Berkley Publishing.
Secrets of Voodoo; Milo Rigaud; Pocket Books.

At the end of the Month an oral test should be given to determine the Neophyte's basic knowledge and familiarity with Craft Traditions.

The entire sixth Month should be taken up by a research project chosen by the Neophyte from any of the reading material covered thus far.

At the end of the Month a basic research. paper should be handed in to the Instructor and a Short talk presented to the class by the Neophyte covering the subject chosen..

The paper should be graded more on the content and the effort put into it by the Neophyte, in his or her research, rather than in being judged for perfection of grammar and/or literary style. Absorption of knowledge is the most important thing to consider.

The first half of the course is complete.

The seventh through the eleventh Month is devoted to the study of basic ESP. It is not the aim of the Grade of Neophyte to master any of the Psychic Sciences in toto. However, a general knowledge of the various fields of Psychism should be the goal.

People develop psychic ability at different speeds and to varying degrees of ability. It is hoped that the course will wet the appetite of the Neophyte sufficiently to study and possibly specialize in one of the psychic fields later on in life.

The High Priesthood and/or Artisan in charge of the Neophytes should hold classes with more "lab work" than lecture during the second half of the course.

The exercises for developing psychic ability may be gleaned from the suggested reading material, explained to the Neophyte and given him or her to practice at home.

Each Month written and oral tests should be held in order to check the progress of the Neophyte in understanding psychic development.

Assimilation of the knowledge and familiarity with the subject material are, however, the prime factors to consider. Rather than expecting the Neophyte to display perfect psychic ability, he or she should be encouraged to seek out the field of psychism that would be best suited for his or her as an individual, always keeping in mind that some persons are not natural psychics and would need considerable time to develop such ability.

There is always a place in the Craft for each person according to his or her own merit.

The development of psychic ability is not a prerequisite to being a Witch. Therefore, the Neophyte should only be presented with the methods to cultivate the different forms of psychism and allowed to seek his or her own level.

The Neophyte should be judged on willingness to experiment with the lessons and willingness to apply the necessary disciplines involved, rather than on success or failure in the display of psychic ability.

Suggested material:

The Astral Plane; Leadbeater; The Theosophical Publishing House.
How to Test and Develop Your ESP; Paul Huson; Stein and Day.
David St. Clair's Lessons in Instant ESP; Prentice Hall Inc.
Astral Doorways; J.H. Brennan; Weiser; N.Y.
Clairvoyance and Occult Powers; Swami Panchadasi; Yogi
    Publication Society.
Psychic Energy; J.J. Weed; Parker Publishing Co.
Thought Power; Annie Besant; Theosophical Publishing House.
The Psychic Healing Book; Wallace and Henkin; Delacorte Press.
The Complete Illustrated Book of the Psychic Sciences; Gibson and
    Gibson; Doubleday.
Master Guide to Psychism; Boswell; Lancer Books..
The Art and Practice of Creative Visualization; Ophiel; Weiser; N.Y.
Methods of Psychic Development; Crawford; Llewellyn.
Creative Visualization; Wiehl; Llewellyn.
The Psychic is You; Rhea; Celestial Arts.
Telepathy; Sybil Leek; Collier Books.
The Diviner's Handbook; Graves; Warner Books.
*How to Read the Aura, Practice Psychometry Telepathy and
    Clairvoyance;* W. E. Butler; Warner Books.
How to Tell Fortunes; Rod Davies; Pinnacle Books.
Palmistry; Mary Anderson; Weiser; N.Y.
Palmistry: The Whole View; Hipskind; Llewellyn.
The Complete Gypsy Fortune Teller; Martin; G. P. Putnam's Sons.

The twelfth Month should be given over to a research project involving some aspect of the Psychic Sciences and a paper written on one subject covered in the second Six Months.

The Neophyte should then be ready to accept the next level of initiation; the Grade of Probationer.

During this year of study, the Neophyte should obtain his or her set of Craft Tools. Those will be needed for him or her to consecrate as part of the lessons in the Grade of Probationer and to employ him or herself during the initiation ceremony attaining the First Degree status as Craftsman.

Magical Axioms Part 1

I. It has been said nothing happens to us we not will to happen. Thus, the witch needs but only to plant a "seed" in people's minds which cause them to dwell upon whatever is to come or upon whatever danger or "ill" has been predicted. Such becomes firmly embedded in the subconscious which in turn directs people's actions to whatever end result the witch presaged; good or bad.

II-A. The name of an object or person contains the essence of the thing or person. To name a substance after a person using the will power to impregnate the substance with thought energy and to visualize an image of the person on the substance, Creates that person's essence within the substance. What is done to the image, is done to the person.

B) In many instances it is better to have a physical link from the subject or victim worked into the substance forming the image. A "tag-lock" of hair, nail clippings, blood or excreta from the body could be employed. Such objects carry the vibrational essence of the person from whom they come, having been in contact with the person in an intimate way. Such an object provides the focal point of concentration for the witch.

C. This is the principle behind the lore of the waxen image; the ancient theory of like to like. That which is done to a replica of a thing is done to the thing itself.

III. The astral plane (gray area) is quite apart from the physical, but names and words have the same vibrational ratios in an archetypal condition. They can serve to link the two planes calling through a "metaphysical" power to accomplish the will of the witch on the physical plane. The gray area encompasses the imagination, and in operating the art magical it is only the personal imagination which triggers powers from the deep mind. If the deep mind has been rightly attuned during the working of a spell or ritual, the subject should feel the effect and show signs thereof within a very few days. It takes time to affect a waking conscious through its own levels of the deep mind via the gray area.

IV-A. The secret of success in working witchcraft rests in whipping up the passions to the correct intensity and at the same time alerting the deep mind by the right degree of concentration and proper numbers of repetitions of the visions and chants.

B. In spellcasting the actual materials used or consumed in themselves are only focal points for the concentration of the deep mind of the practitioner. It is the intent, the force of will and the attitude behind that will which makes a spell effective.

C. For love spells the emotion should be real toward the subject. The desires and even lust must be turned up to the point of orgasm or climax, which releases a bioelectrical energy from the spellcaster.

D. For curses and spells of vengeance the emotions of hatred and violence must be whipped up and sent forth in a repetitious ritual until a point of utter physical exhaustion has been reached.

E. Power manifests where attention is directed.

V-A. By chant, sonically, of a word or name, the higher form of that "idea" can be magically contacted. Each thought, idea or action carried out on the physical plane sets off a sympathetic response on the astral or gray area.

B. When casting a spell, vibrations are set off by the witch's thoughts, words and actions which contact the astral essence of the person on whom the spell is cast, causing a response accordingly. The one affected by the spell will react actively to do things to him or herself as the spellcaster wishes.

VI-A. In order to affect a thing over distances of time and space, one must have intense concentration and be actually "obsessed" with the idea of that which one wishes to affect. The stronger the feelings, the more intense the vibrations eminating from the mind. A state of "frenzy" would be the easiest picture one could give to describe such state of mind.

B) Repetition of the ritual is also important. The more often repeated, the stronger the will power and the subconscious would become.

Magical Axioms Part II

I. All of creation is composed of vibrations which proceed from the unknowable eternal infinite we call God/Goddess. They penetrate the layers of matter from the most rarified and refined to the densest. The reactions of these vibrations upon the matter in the densest layer produce the physical universe. They vibrate through eons of time in all the planes of being in their cycle both from and to whence they came.

II. The being "man" is a four-planed entity. He has a physical element, an astral counterpart, a reasoning mentality and a spiritual core.

III. The astral plane contains man's thoughts, emotions and desires. These attract around themselves the subtle matter of that plane. That matter is plastic and assumes the form of the thought which is projected into it.

IV. The astral plane was called such by the witches of old due to its luminosity having a higher rate of vibration than the physical. It is chiefly this plane the witch deals with in works of the art magic.

V. On the astral a person is seen only by his/her aura; a large pentagram, according to the hermetic philosophy. Most persons thoughts are weak, cling close to the aura of their creator and dissipate after a time. The more intense and more detailed last longer and eminate further afield. They can lose themselves in the aura of the one they are sent to affect, causing, thereupon, a sympathetic response.

Magical Axioms Part III

I. Your word will not return unto your void.

II. Thoughts are things. Thoughts are the stepping stones to knowledge, and knowledge is power.

III. Evil has no power apart from what you give it by believing in it.

IV. Whatever you believe with great emotion, that you will bring into your life by the use of creative imagination. The perfect prayer or meditation is the method to bring this about. For whatever you need, or for that very special need, meditate and give the need to the divine creative intelligence and then forget it immediately. You will receive what you asked for in the form you are prepared to receive it.

V. Creative thought is a mental branding-iron. When you want something for yourself, mentally brand it with your name and it will be yours.

VI. Man is a mental being and mind is primary. Mind is cause and experience is effect. Change the cause and the right experience will follow. Your thoughts materialize as experience weaving the pattern of your destiny.

VII. Before a thought pattern or a creative idea can work in your life, it must be accepted by your subconscious mind. Repetition of an idea conditions the subconscious to accept it. Build by use of picture images in the subconscious those experiences which will later materialize as physical reality.

VIII. Think it, talk it, live it and it will materialize. What you bind in your belief will be bound and what you loose with the same conviction, will be loosed.

IX. Use your mind and your will power. Learn to control and focus your thoughts. Whatever you give your mind and attention to, you will become and whatever you concentrate your will power upon will come into your life.

X. Emotional control and release are necessary in the practice of the art magical. Control for visualizing the effect you want to produce and emotional surge to propel toward the subject of your working.

THE BOOK OF THE WISE III

THE SACRED TOOLS OF THE CRAFT

Study guide for the grade of Probationer leading to
initiation as a Craftsman I° Witch.

Tarostar V°
Magister Sacrorum
Circle of Starmeadow
Ancient Order of Bell Book and Candle, Las Vegas, Nevada

The Grade of Probationer is assumed during the initiation ceremony bestowed on the Vernal Equinox one year hence from becoming a Neophyte. Thereupon, the Probationer should begin to study for the next Level of Initiation, approximately Six Months later. The third level grants the individual the actual status as a Witch; Craftsmen First Degree.

As the Probationer prepares for the First Degree Ceremony, he or she continues to attend the classes given by the High Priesthood. This series of study is to cover the basic groundwork in the understanding of magical methods.

The suggested reading material should be digested by the Probationer and discussed in class with the High Priesthood. No written tests need be given. However, the instructors are to tell from the discussions of magical philosophy, how well the Probationer has absorbed the material.

The real work of the Probationer is in the planning and conducting of the brief rituals for the consecration of his or her own Sacred Tools preparatory to employing them during the 1st Degree Initiation.

The High Priesthood assigns reading for discussion from such works as the following:

Philosophy of the Magical Elements and Correspondences:
Magic, an Occult Primer; Conway; E. P. Dutton.
Magical Ritual Methods; W.G. Gray; Helios.

Inner Traditions of Magic; W.G. Gray: Weiser.
The Tree of Life: A Study in Magic; Israel Regardie; Weiser.
The Magician: His Training and Work; W. E. Butler; Wilshire Books.
Incantations and Words of Power; E. Maple; Weiser.
The Practice of Ritual Magic; G. Knight; Weiser.
Occult Exercises and Practices; G. Knight; Weiser.

The traditions of candleburning:
Candleburning: Its Occult Significance; M. Howard; Weiser.
The Magic Candle; C. Dey; Original Products; N.Y.
Candle Magic; Leo Vinci; The Aquarian Press.
Practical Candleburning Ritual; Ray Buckland; Llewellyn.

Preparatory Divination:
Tarot; Connally; Newcastle Publishing Co.
The Devil's Picture Book; Paul Huson; G.P. Putnam & Sons.
A Practicle Guide to Geomantic Divination; Israel Regardie; Weiser.
Magic Mirrors; N. Clough; Weiser.

General theory:
The Complete Book of White Magic; K. Martin; A.S. Barnes & Co.;
    London
The Complete Book of Spells, Ceremonies and Magic; Gonzalez;
    Wippler, Crown Publishers.

This series of lessons should consume the six Months following the initiation to Probationer. He or she should read and study the works assigned and be able to answer any quiz or oral exam that the High Priesthood may give in their discussion classes.

In the meantime, the Probationer is proceeding with the practicle application of the rituals which follow. In Other words, it takes a period of 18 Months to obtain the status of Craftsman First Degree and to become a Witch.

The Ceremonies for The Sacred Tools

To Consecrate an Athamé

After the initiation to Probationer level, at which time the Craft tools are presented to the Initiate, he or she must begin to gather the needed supplies for these rituals. (All the Witch's Sacred Tools must he consecrated and charged properly before the Probationer advances to become a Witch by taking the First Degree Initiation.)

Some traditions call for the Athamé to be buried in the Earth for a period of time to receive its consecration. The Way of the Wise, however, feels such is wrong.

Never is anything to be consecrated by burial in the Earth. She is destructive in that She claims everything unto Herself. She will only cause the metallic substance to discharge and begin to oxydize, even if set upon Her for a short while.

Therefore, any Tool of the Craft to be used in "The Art Magical" must be insulated from the Earth Element by a linen cloth whenever placed upon Her to magnetize.

On a Day of Mars as Luna wanes the knife chosen as an Athame is annealed with Fire and Water to "Make it virgin" by being heated to a cherry glow with a blow torch or in the embers of a fire. It is then plunged into a bucket of water to realign its molecular structure.

Out of doors upon the Earth, the knife is placed on a linen cloth with blade pointing North and a small magnet set at both ends for 24 hours. (The waning Moon is best for this work because this is the Witch Weapon with which most banishings are performed and the will of the Witch is imposed upon places and things).

On the following Day of Mars as Luna wanes, this consecration is performed:

A small home Altar is erected and covered with a red cloth.

A Waning Moon symbol is painted on the blade's black handle in white. Any other symbols would be optional.

The Athamé is placed in the center of the Altar, blade to the North. West of it is placed some salted water. To the East is set a dish of burning Martial Incense. North of the blade should be a vial of Sacred

Oil, while to the South stands a lit red candle.

The Altar is circumambulated 13 times widdershins, as these words are spoken:

Athamé, Blade of the Craft, be pure and virgin, blessed by earth.

The salted water is sprinkled thrice upon the blade as these words are said:

Waters of emotional love empower this blade to work for me, blessed be!

The athamé is taken up and wiped dry with a clean cloth and passed thrice through the incense smoke with these words:

Fire and Air command this blade to work my will, blessed be!

A dab of Sacred Oil is placed upon the blade handle as its secret name is whispered over it. (Henceforth, never is that name to be mentioned, or its power will be lost.)

The Athamé is taken up in the right hand and the candle in the left. The blade and candle are held crosswise together forming a barrier cross as this Charge is spoken:

Witches Blade work for me.
Never blood of man you'll see.
Pure and true you banish all evil
and astral phantoms of the mind primeval.
Rule all elements of this world,
to impose my will as a banner unfurled,
blessed be!

The barrier cross composed of knife and candle is then circumambulated thrice around the altar with these words:

Banish adversity, banish all woe.
Impose my will as around we go. Blessed be!

The blade and candle are set back down upon the altar and the candle allowed to burn out. The Athamé rests there for 24 hours.

The blade is then wrapped in linen and placed away for future use.

The Athamé will first be employed by the Probationer when called upon to cast his/her own Magic Circle during the First Degree Initiation Ceremony.

THE LORE OF THE BLADE

In Magical Tradition the Witch's Blade is used to impose Will upon things and places in time and space. It helps to erect Psychic barriers and create astral thought forms placed upon the Etheric Realms by the mind and Will of the Witch or Wizard. Much practice goes into developing that ability.

Practice by placing a spot on a blank wall about eye level. Stand before it about four feet away and concentrate on the spot. Bring the blade up to stab the center of the spot without touching the wall.

In other words, be able to stick the point of the blade forcefully into any form seen held in mind. Drive the blade to the heart of the vision held in mind. The flow of the gesture should be quick and decisive. With practice, the blade can flow to its astral target without hesitation or conscious effort.

Next practice drawing and imposing Invoking and Banishing Pentagrams in and on the Ether of space before you. The flow of the blade should be quick and fast, leaving an astral impression, held in mind, of a Pentagram Symbol in space before your eyes.

An invoking Pentagram sets up a widdershins force flow of energy to bring in the Magical Powers or Entities called upon.

A Banishing Pentagram turns the astral or Etheric in a deosil fashion to drive out or away any force already there.

With practice, the gestures will become second nature and be done without effort.

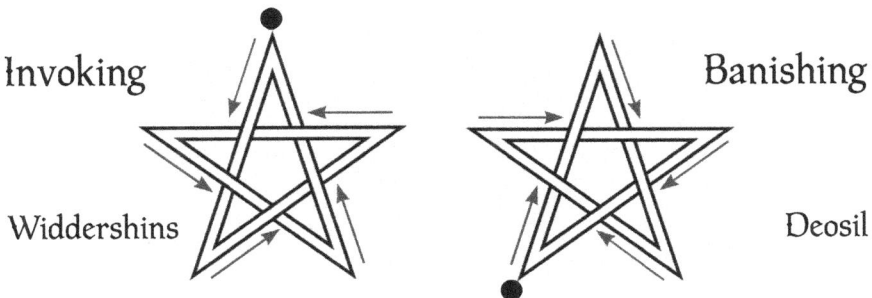

Invoking

Widdershins

Banishing

Deosil

Ritual to Consecrate a Witch's Chalice

The Chalice is consecrated on a Day and Hour of Venus; during the waxing phase of the Moon.

The altar is set with a green cloth and a lit green taper candle set at the North edge.

Set a Venus Incense to burn at the East edge of the altar with a cup of salted water to the West. Set a dish of salt to the North next to the candle.

When this has been done, bring the Chalice to the altar, raise it high to the North and bow. Sprinkle it silently with a few drops of the salted water as you think of it being washed clean of all previous associations. Then wipe the Chalice dry with a clean cloth.

Next pass it thrice though the incense smoke as you silently dedicate it to your works of magic.

Take the Chalice in both hands and hold it to your heart as you proceed to walk 7 times widdershins around the altar humming a lullaby to the Chalice, as though it were a Human Child. (The lullaby should be either one from your own childhood, or one made up on the spot as long as it has happy emotional connotations.)

Then take the dish of salt and sprinkle a large circle in the center of the altar deosil. Then make a smaller widdershins circle within that. Set the Chalice within the two salt circles.

Extend your hands above it in the attitude of blessing and say:

Womb of Mystery, Cup of Life,
bring happy emotions and block out strife.
Be my symbol of the moving sea,
to rule the waters along with me. Blessed be, O Emotion's Frame,
encompass love in the Goddess's name.

The Chalice is left to stand in the center of the altar for 24 hours within the salt circles and the taper left to burn out.

It should then be wrapped in linen and placed away for future use, first during the First Degree Ceremony.

THE LORE OF THE CHALICE

The Chalice standing for the Water Element has come to be associated with the mysterious Holy Grail. It rules the desires and the emotional realm in Magical Tradition.

It also is associated with Psychic fluidity and acts as the Magic Mirror for the Art of Scrying,

In order to develop the rudimentary Psychic ability, it is necessary to train one's mind to attain a calm, unemotional state of hopeful expectation. From that center point in consciousness, concentration on a question or problem can bring visions and impressions to the mind.

The Astrological force called Mercury rules the Psychic and it is during the times of mercurial influence that one may obtain better psychic impressions. For purposes of scrying, use the Days or Nights of Mercury, as the Moon waxes in an Air sign to read visions and impressions seen in the water of the Chalice.

Ring the Chalice with 8 candles of yellow or light blue.

Set a pleasant incense of Benzoin or Sandalwood to burn.

Light the candles around the Chalice of Water moving widdershins, counter-clockwise.

Calm the mind and concentrate on a specific question, without straining or effort. This will help open the Psychic channels to the divinatory powers. Allow the vision produced in the sparkling reflections of the candles upon the water to speak to your inner mind as they will.

With time, adepthood in scrying will be properly developed so as to make one a good Psychic Reader.

The Chalice is also used in works of the amatory nature in casting Love Spells. It is used to conjure visions of the face of the intended lover onto the surface of the water in order to influence him/her on the emotional level.

Fridays as the Moon waxes in a Water Sign would be the best time for those kinds of works. Through a vivid image of the lover, one has access to the deep levels of mind.

To Consecrate The Thurible

An altar Thurible is a small bowl or cauldron holding sand or rocks in order to insulate burning coals and incense from scorching during rituals as they are burned.

Pick a Day of Mercury during the waxing tide of the Moon and at the exact moment of Dawn, which is the Hour of Mercury.

Have these things arranged near an open window facing East, or out of doors, to catch the Sunrise.

A yellow cloth is to be laid out flat on the floor or ground. Upon it place 3 yellow candles as a triangle with its apex to the East. At the West edge of the cloth have a cup of salted Water.

To the South of the triangle place your flint and steel (cigarette lighter). To the North of the triangle set a dish of salt.

The Thurible rests within the triangle half filled with sand (also coals and a Mercurial Incense rest nearby).

At the exact moment of Sunrise, when it lifts its crown above the horizon, light the yellow candles and say:

Greetings Sol, the Earth salutes thee.
Bless this Mercurial Magic at this hour.
The Sacred Elements Four aid me in this
work of power. Blessed be!

Stand up and begin to walk deosil around the objects arranged upon the cloth as you chant:

Sol and Hermes, Appollo and Mercury, Balder and Odin, Ra and
Thoth, names from times forgotten and ages of ages. From children's
fables with dusty pages, praised and sung by the Ancient Sages.
Heat and motion, light and life,
banishes inertia and casts out strife. Magics and auguries and
forecasts dire, the psychic element my soul doth inspire.
In Mercury's tide
shall magic bide
to banish evil

and force it to hide.
Blessed be this sacred time
to the Horned One and the Goddess sublime.

After the objects have been circumambulated 8 times, the salt is taken up and sprinkled around the triangle of candles deosil to form a circle and these words spoken:

Spheres of stars and spheres of cycles, ever onward the
ancient duality.
The Circle is our ordered symbol, by it we measure human
mortality.

The water is exchanged for the salt and a few drops are sprinkled on the Thurible as these words are spoken:

The sea is love, the sea gives life.
Fluidity added to mentality
makes us strong unto finality.

The Water is replaced on the Altar Cloth. Then the coal and incense are taken up. The coal is lit and placed upon the sand in the Thurible. As a few grains of the incense is cast upon it, these words are said, as the smoke rises:

Fumes and smoke,
fragrance and cense,
to thwart all evil and send it hence.
Fumes and cense,
fragrance and smoke
draw in the good
as blessings be spoke.

The hands are placed above the Thurible in the smoke in an attitude of blessing as the Charge is given:

Censer, censer, incense burner, imprisoned within this salt
Circle white.
Give forth your blessings with delight.

As you stand within this ring, create a Circle about all Magic
rites where you are used.
Draw an air of blessings for each and every work of power.
Rule the airy forces by
Mercury's swift and Magic might. Blessed be, O King of Air!

The Thurible is lifted up and presented to the 4 Quarters widdershins beginning in the East and censing thrice to each Quarter silently. A final censing is made toward the Sunrise and the Thurible replaced within the 3 candles. All candles and incense are left to burn themselves out. Then clean the Thurible and put it away for future use.

If this is done out of doors, do not scatter the salt from off the cloth onto the ground. It will kill any living thing and make the Earth barren in that spot. Dispose of it some other way.

To Consecrate The Altar Pentacle
The Craft Earth Symbol

The Pentacle is either a small flat round dish to contain salt or earth during rituals, or a. flat piece of stone, wood or wax, upn which a small dish containing those items would stand.

Consecrate the Pentacle on a Day and Hour of Saturn as the Moon Waxes.

An upright Pentagram should be inscribed on it in either black or silver.

The altar should also be covered with black or silver and bear 10 brown candles arranged in a circle evenly spaced.

A burner with live coal for the Earth Incense (Patchouli, Musk or Kyphi) will set at the East edge of the altar. A cup of salted water will stand in the West.

When the altar has been thus arranged, the Pentacle is taken out of doors into the open air, held high to the North as these words are spoken:

Mother Earth, come bless this shield,
be it a symbol of our Solid World.

A bow is given to the North and the Pentacle taken back to the altar.

It is placed in the center of the unlit circle of candles. Set the incense to the coal in the burner and rap upon the altar 10 times and speak these words:

Summon to me, summon to me,
the powers in the Earth that be,
ten is your number.
I arouse you from slumber.
Blessed be this Earth rite
in the gracious Goddess's sight.

The Pentacle is picked up and passed through the incense 10 times as these words are spoken into the rising smoke:
Fragrance of Earth fill your frame
to shield my Magic in the Goddess's name.

A few drops of the salted water are sprinkled on the Pentacle, as the following words are spoken:

The Earth contains the Sea.
The Ocean floods the Earth.
Cycles and Ages and Eons that be.
You are the Goddes's bejeweled girth.
Blessed be!

The Pentacle is then replaced in the circle of candles and the candles are lit widdershins starting in the North with the traditional "Earth Fire" of flint and steel (modern cigarette lighter).

As the fire surrounds the Pentacle and burns brightly, the hands are held above the circle of candles and the Charge spoken thus:

O Pentacle, O Pentacle, Shield of Magic,
symbol of Earth,
the gracious Goddess gives you birth.
Safe within the Earth Fire's womb
you mark the times
and the Earth's silent forces you disentomb.
I charge you to rule the kingdom of

the Crystal Forces, the rocks and elements of
solid things,
all which solidity and stability brings.

Ten more raps are made upon the altar and the candles are left to
burn themselves out.

The Pentacle rests there for 24 hours, Then wrap it up and put it
away for the future.

The candle wax and incense ashes must be scattered on the Earth
at that time.

The Altar Pentacle

SPELLS OF THE CORNUCOPIA

Dedicated and recommended to those aspiring to Artisan II° status as, Priest/Priestess of the Ancient Craft in the Way of the Wise. The spell, or the consecration of a Talisman to be performed in full Coven by the Candidate to II° status, may be chosen from any collection and from any tradition of the Occult Arts. These, the Cornucopia, are offered as suggestions.

INTRODUCTION

A Covenstead is the center of our group religious expression. It is the Temple, the Ritual Chamber, the hearthfire of The Old Religion.

We will not concern ourselves with what Covens may or may not have done in previous Centuries and Ages. In many instances, continuity of practice can not be clearly traced and established beyond doubt, due to the dearth of evidence allowed to filter down to Modern Times.

All we can say for sure, is that people have adhered to the old ways of popular religious practice above and beyond and outside of the "Official Cult", which, in the Western World, is Christianity, since times long past.

The Humanism of the "Pagan" Past is in resurgence in this time period. The Official Cult, maintained by Government, State and Church, no longer holds sway over intelligent hearts and minds.

The Old Religion, therefore, seeks the light of Religious Freedoms secured by Law and ancient practice. It may now bring forth more of its inner light and Wisdom Religion.

This section, *Spells of The Cornucopia,* is designed to give a more accurate picture to the observances and rites conducted by a well run Coven in the ideal of Wicca/Old Religion.

It is to help Witches/Pagans, observing the true essence of Wicca, have a set of Temple Ceremonies, of a minor order, to practice, which with time, build up a reservoir of vibrational energies, making the Covenstead very spiritual and potent as well.

Ritual purity can not be over-stated in The Old Religion. Rites performed for periods of time, over and over, as necessary, impress upon the spiritual ethers an identifying code, so to speak, which helps attract the Orders of beings above the Physical and the Nature Entities as well.

They would attend, on the inner planes and lend their force and powers to the Rites, Ceremonies and Magics engaged in by a Coven. They must not be ignored, nor forgotten.

They are recognized and given a small offering before major Sabbats. Consider them the "Penates" of Classical Times. It is for them, these minor rites are performed to preserve the potency of the Ritual Atmosphere in a Temple or Covenstead. Neglected, the life, the inner feeling of religious observances, is not there.

It is a spiritually vibrational feeling these minor Covenstead Rites are designed to create and maintain within the Ritual Chambers of The Old Religion. It had that feeling in the Ancient Past, and would strive to re-create it today.

A place becomes consecrated by its habitual use, not by "Holy Words" spoken by some priest or Hierophant. A true Temple of the Old Gods would give one that special consecrated feeling by merely walking into it.

It is very important in Ritual Work to have the correct atmosphere for the power of the Gods to manifest and work its blessings in and upon those who seek their Light and Love.

Used wisely, the Old Religion will speak for itself.

PREPARATION TIME

Many books are written on Spellcraft and Magic and offer various kinds of procedures to follow. However, very little space is devoted to the most important aspect of success in the Occult.

Some read a spell and jump in trying to do it on the drop of a hat. Some have created such powerful occult and spooky reputations for themselves by impressing the impressionable, that they feel they can dispense with necessary preparation time altogether.

Does any star or professional entertainer refrain from rehearsal? How many hours of private rehearsal go into a public performance of any kind?

The same is of the utmost importance for works of Magic.

One must first decide what type of Magic Ritual or Spell would be needed for a particular situation and then calculate the most propitious and corresponding astrological configurations for it. One must know when the tides are right, in order to have the flow of the Cosmos/ Universal Flux, going with, not against nor transverse to, one's magics.

Hypothetically, let us say it is a Waning Moon, Day of Mercury, Moon in an Earth Sign.

The Occult Shop Apothecary probably is not doing much in the line of business, so, he/she tells a customer: "Oh, yes, today is just fabulous for a Love Spell! You will need ...." , just to make any sale possible.

The customer, if not up on astrological knowledge, would buy and work it and wonder why nothing happened. Wrong tide, time and day! Go ahead and swim upstream, if you will, but by working with the flow, in proper order, success will come with less effort.

By setting the proper time in the future, from a good Ephemeris or an Astrological Calendar, one has days to set about gathering the needed ingredients for the Spell or Ritual.

One then thinks it out clearly, lives it in mind, stages it in one's consciousness, thinks it, feels it and knows it to such a detailed degree, that when the Spell or Ritual act is finally performed on the proper day or night, the ceremony is but the climax - release - for and of all the steamed up energy built in and during the preparation time. The Magic then has every omen for positive results.

If you think you can just flip your finger and have Magic happen, you have been watching too many movies!!!!

If you think you can prance around in a Magic Circle and scream at the Gods and demand your Will be done, you've missed the boat somewhere along the line. Yet, that is often what we see "Magickians" trying to do. They attempt to overcome lack of preparation by sheer expenditure of energy.

God/Goddess are Principle, not Personality. You could not influence them, nor insult them, no matter what you did. The Course of the Cosmos will not change. However, one can cause changes in situations according to one's Will, which is Magic, when one works with the Astrological Tides, set by the Godhead.

The Gods manifest through the principles of what we know as Astrology. Calculate the most favorable transits and aspects for your

Magics. That is why Preparation Time must not be ignored. To do so is folly.

Traditionally, the Astrological Forces of the Planets imprint an essence or a "vibe", if you will, to the days of the week. Each day of the week bears a personal association with the Planet which governs it. The Planet rules certain aspects of Human physical and spiritual activities.

SUN	Sunday	Honors, Wealth, Health, Advancement, Good Fortune.
MOON	Monday	Peace, The Subconscious, Emotional Affinity, Illusions.
VENUS	Friday	Harmony, Friendships, Love, Beauty, Artistic Expression.
MARS	Tuesday	Strife, War, Justice and Defense. Sex and Passion.
MERCURY	Wednesday	Psychism, Divinations, Luck, Gambling, Business.
JUPITER	Thursday	Expansion, Prosperity, Fortunes and Magnanimity.
SATURN	Saturday	Lessons, Karma, Limitations, Restrictions.

The positive or the negative applications of those main qualities affect the individual day.

With the Waxing Moon, and with the Planet in favorable aspect to Her and to other Planets, brings out the positive side of the Planetary Nature. The Waning Moon and/or adverse aspects of the Planets to Her and to each other, would allow a negative or a stressful situation to affect the day.

Also the Nature of the Zodiac Sign in which the Moon passes mutates the vibrational energies and affects them either positively or negatively. The Element of a Sign would cast a specific quality onto the day: Fire, Water, Air or Earth.

Magic has been, for millennia, associated with the Power of the Lunar Tides. Her influence has the most active and direct bearing on the type and kind of Magic to be cast on any particular Day.

The Covenstead should have a competent grounding in Astrology to be able to apply the qualifying astrological associations in working Magic.

One must know the nature of a Waxing Moon in each and every Sign and in aspect to the Planets as they transit. Obversely, the affect of the Waning Tide must also be studied as the Moon passes in Signs and in aspect.

Then, favorable days can be calculated upon which the Coven could work Spellcraft and conduct Ceremonial Ritual. Every Coven should have one or two persons well versed in Astrology.

The astrological calculations would be one of the first steps in the total over all Preparation Time invested in any work of Spellcraft.

A Natural Zodiac Wheel for the Heavens can he drawn for any day and the Transiting Planets placed in the proper Signs, so that the mutating affects of the Moon, in waxing or waning phase, can be seen. This map of the Heavens would show, by study of the interconnecting influences of the Planets and the Moon, how the particular day/night would stack up for particular works of Spellcraft or Ritual.

One just does not decide to do a Spell and ignore the important powers exerted by the Astrological Configurations and expect to have success. The flow of energy and the flavor of the Tide must be taken into intelligent consideration. At least, those of the Craft do so.

THE WITCH'S CANDLE BLESSING

It is in the best of magical traditions to bless candles before they are employed in a Spell or Ritual. The reason being, they are composed of natural substances which catch and hold a magnetic charge from the minds and attitudes of those around them.

Candles sit around factories, truck loading docks and for long periods of time on Occult Shop shelves. They will assume the "vibes"/influences from those persons who are habitually around them and from those who pick up and handle them.

One would want to ensure the candle has a state of virginal purity before one would apply it in a magic working of any sort. The candle must be dedicated to the Witch's or the Practitioner's Magic Will alone.

For that reason, candles should be ritually blessed to cleanse and purify them of any previous associations, once they are bought and brought to the Covenstead for use in Spellcraft.

This minor blessing is good ritual practice and should be done to each fresh batch of candles to be used in Magic.

Light a white candle and place a Goblet of water next to it. On the other side of the candle set a sweet Incense to burn.

Place the candle(s) to be blessed to rest before the burning white candle.

Set a dish of salt before the candle(s).

Take up the candle(s) to be blessed in the strongest hand and with the mind, see all negative associations fleeing from you and the candle. Say:

In the Name of the God and Goddess, I cleanse, purify and cast out any adverse conditions which may linger here. Blessed be!

Pass the candle(s) right through the flame of the white candle and pass it/them then through the Incense smoke.

Then, with the candle(s) still in the strongest hand, sprinkle some water out of the goblet onto the candle(s) and also cast a few grains of salt onto it/them. Say:

I bless, consecrate and ratify this/these wax candle(s) to the Magic Work of this Coven. Blessed be!

Set the candle(s) down upon the Altar or work space and place both hands over them in an attitude of blessing and say:

May the Powers of this Coven's Magic be the only force absorbed by and worked through this/these candle(s).
Blessed be!

The candle(s) may then be locked away out of sight to be kept for future use as needed in Spells and Rituals.

That is the general format for taper and jumbo sized candles. Those in the glass jars should be washed outside and around the inner rim of the glass with isopropal alcohol before being blessed. That clears away any excess wax drippings on the glass jar.

One must present one's best efforts to the Gods/Astrological Forces as valuable attention to detail in magical purity. Haphazard or sloppy attitudes and neglect of correct procedures only tells the Forces that be, that one is not putting out one's best efforts to gain the request/ prayer, Spell or Ritual. One would only get same from them in return.

THE CIRCLE OF ART

The Witch's Magic Space, wherein the acts of Spellcraft are done, has traditionally been associated with what has come to be called the Magic Circle of Art.

It is somewhat different from a Sabbat Circle for Worship and from an Esbat Circle for Coven Magics. This Circle deals with the forces of Magic which the individual Witch/Practitioner conjures and/or evokes just for his/her own personal Spells and Rituals.

It contains the energy the Witch evokes to send and accomplish his/her Will, or it forms a barrier in which the Practitioner of the Arcane Arts summons forces from the Unseen Beyond.

The most convenient Altar Space would simply be a black cloth spread upon the floor or Earth in the center of the work area. The Circle itself would be large enough to allow the Witch room in which to move around, generally 9 ft. in diameter.

The Tools of Art would then be arranged upon the cloth in the center along with the necessary items for the Spell or Ritual at hand.

There would be a Thurible for the Incense corresponding to the Spell standing at the East side, a Chalice of water at the West, a Pentacle for salt or Earth at the North and a small candle for Fire at the South along with the Athamé (or Sword, should the Witch be III°).

Within the center, between the tools, would rest whatever items a Spell may call to use.

At the appointed time for the work, the Tools and necessary items are placed upon the cloth. The candle is lit and the Incense burning. The Witch would then proceed to Cast the Circle:

Taking up the Incense in the Thurible, it is circumambulated around the area widdershins in silence as a wish is made to clear a space for Magic. Replacing the Incense, the blade and candle are taken up and also circumambulated North to North. As the blade is carried around, an Invoking Pentagram is inscribed in the Air at each Quarter with these words:

Powers of the Four Mighty Ones, bless this Work by air and fire. Build my Inner Temple of Art. Be it strong and sound of purpose.

After all Quarters have been thus addressed, North to North, the candle and blade are put back in place.

A firm commanding attitude should be displayed by the Witch at all times which impresses the power onto the Ether.

The Spell or Ritual may then be cast.

Afterwards, the Circle has to be taken down in a reverse manner:

The Chalice of Water is circumambulated around the Circle, North to North, deosil as a banishing Pentagram is inscribed in the Air holding the Chalice firm and upright (the Chalice is used to form the Pentagram). Then a few drops of Water are scattered to each Quarter with these words:

Powers of the Four Mighty Ones, bless this Work by water and earth. Be all forces sent away. Let normal time and space prevail.

The Chalice is then replaced by the dish of salt or Earth and a few grains scattered around the Circle in silence deosil.

The Witch/Practitioner may then depart the Circle area.

This basic format should be learned by rote so that it can be performed for each work of Spellcraft where a Magic Circle is required.

THE HERBAL LOVE POTION

This is a work of Venus, Planetary Influence for Love. It should be done on a Friday Night as the Moon waxes. If She waxes in a Water Sign, that is good for emotional harmony, in a Fire Sign, for passion and sex, in an Air Sign for mental stimulation and friendships, in an Earth Sign for the fertile and material aspects of Love.

In addition to the usual Tools of Art, there should be a Chalice of rich red wine, Incense of Rose or Sandalwood and a pink candle anointed with a Lovers Oil. Have a Mortar and Pestle handy.

To that add 1/4 oz. each of Verbena, Spearmint and Jasmine.

The Circle of Art should be properly cast (see *Circle of Art*). The candle used for the Spell is also the candle used to cast the Circle, as well as the Incense called for.

Place the candle next to the Chalice of Wine and begin to grind the herbs together in the Mortar and Pestle with these words:

Herbs of the Venus Power,
upon my lover all delight I do shower.
Let the one who drinketh of thee,
come to love and be with me!

Chant over and over again as the herbs are thoroughly ground and mixed. The entire area should resonate and vibrate to the sound of the chant.

After a good twenty minutes of grinding and chanting, stare deep into the flame of the candle and see the Lover's face in the flame.

When the image can be held in mind, transfer it to the surface of the wine in the Chalice and say:

_____ , Thou art mine to be.
Thy face in the wine I see.
None but the forces of Love consume thee!
Thou canst not resist. Thou art mine forever!

Cast the herbs into the wine and allow them to steep. (Cover the Chalice with a clean cloth and allow it to steep for 24 hours.)

Close the Circle and clear all away. The candle and Incense should burn themselves out.

On the next day, the wine should be filtered from the Chalice and placed into a stoppered bottle to be put into whatever food or drink one would share with the lover at the next opportunity.

Tradition says soon the lover will turn to thee.

KING SOLOMON'S APPLE LOVE SEAL

(From traditional sources)

If there is to be a Handfasting at the Covenstead, the High Priestess would do this work sufficiently ahead of time to have the necessary tides and astrological forces working to bless the couple.

On a Night of Venus, as the Moon waxes in a Water or Earth Sign, the seal must be scribed in inks of copper brown and reddish pink. The names of the two to be joined in Holy Union by Rite of Handfesting would be scribed on the reverse side.

Seven pink candles are anointed with Lotus Oil and set in a circle around the Seal. A bit of "Love" Incense of Rose and Benzoin would be lit.

She would then burn one candle per night, along with some of the Incense for the seven nights following.

She would chant over and over the seal seven times each night, as the candle burns:

This Seal I bind to handfast these two.
Naught but words of Will will do:
Oyoth, hean, vean, eant!
This couple never shall know want. Wisdom of Sages and
powers of ages,
keep secure as the outside storm rages.
Bless this union bound with love,
Holy Lady high above!

At the Handfasting, she will circumambulate the couple thrice and again recite the sealing words. The couple would keep the Seal as a memento of the Rites.

The Arts of Divination

I. Reading The Aura

This is a very ancient method of Divination used by Wizards from the dim past and time immemorial. It requires a sensitivity to the eminations given off by objects that were in close proximity to a Subject for a time.

Make for yourself two strings of beads and pass them through the smoke of an incense of Benzoin eight times on a Night of Mercury as Luna waxes in an Air Sign.

Thereafter, on Days of Mercury, read for people by having them place a piece of jewelry or trinket worn by them into the center of the two stings of beads.

Intently gaze at the item and allow your sensitivity to seek a rapport with the item and read out what impressions thy inner eye receives therefrom.

II. Cartomancy For The Witch

The ability to function at some form of psychic science is the first basic achievement for those who aspire to mastery in the Craft.

One sees numerous "Readers" advertised all over the World. Mostly in the Tarot Cards.

Tarot Is concerned with the spiritual progress of the Querent for whom its arcana are laid.

All one can say is *Caveat Emptor.*

The playing cards do not presume to take such a responsibility.

They show only the three major human concerns; Love, Luck and Money.

One should be well warned not to place a dependency on a professional "Reader" to the exclusion of common sense.

It would be worth the effort to develop a reading ability of one's own.

Be that as it may, playing cards, as tools for fortunetelling, can be the best way to help one develop the rudimentary psychic ability.

When two persons come together for any reason, the electromagnetic fields of each person's auras merge to produce a temporary Over-Soul which is composed of the best and worst of each being. That merger is what allows the flow of psychic energy to pass between both parties. It is also in contact with the consciousness of the entire human race and its reservoir of knowledge. This may sound rather Jungian but it is more scientific than attributing psychism to nebulous "Spirit Guides".

Psychism is a fluid force. Never try to make it fit any pattern. It must have the freedom to be what it is needed to be for any given person seeking to learn what it can show. If the spontaneous flow is made to conform to a pattern, it will appear to dry up.

That is why there is really no set meaning to the cards. Each author can only give his/her personal opinions as to what any card means for readings.

Meditate on the pattern in each card and allow the card to tell you what it should mean.

Write down each impression and boil that down to a few "key" phrases. In that way you become your own authority on the cards.

I offer my interpretations of the cards as a guideline only. You may use these meanings, however, do not consider them absolute. You may find the cards saying things of their own as you read for any given person.

Allow the Querent to shuffle at least thrice, as he/she concentrates on what is to be known.. I find it best for the Reader not to be told so the cards can read only the Querent's situation. The Reader only interprets the cards as they fall. The Querent fits that meaning into his/her own life or circumstance.

Above all, be only a Medium through which psychic insight may channel. Realize that knowledge comes through you, not from you.

Beware of the temptation to act as an Oracle and bask in the adulation others may place on you when your insights prove true. Leave that form of egotism to those who need to display it.

A Witch develops the "Second Sight" to help fellow beings, but only as a stepping stone on the road back to the realms of spiritual perfection. As time goes by, he/she should grow beyond the "Show and Tell" stage of Spiritual Enlightenment.

Do not consider the playing cards any way inferior to the Tarot.

They give practical advise not spiritual. You are functioning as a Fortuneteller, not a metaphysical adviser.

Read the cards honestly, be sensitive to the Querent and keep the mind open to feelings and impressions as they flow through you.

Avoid the situation of allowing a Querent to affix a dependency on "Readings", where he/she would request a Reading almost every other day. Some will be impressed with your ability and wish to ask your advise before (proverbially) going to the bathroom.

Know what power that places in your hands. The Lords of Karma will not be cheated.

A Witch is about the only honest Psychic one can find in these days of wrath and anguish, days of calamity and misery. Be honest. In that way the Arts of Divination are used as they should be, as an aid to help the lost navigate properly through the stormy sea of life. No more, no less.

Suit of Hearts

ACE: "The romantic card." *The promise of joy.* It is the cause for celebration. Love versus sex. Good feelings about the matter. An indication, of good news concerning an emotional relationship or romantic love. A birth or rebirth of spiritual faith and joy. It indicates a better social life. *The basis for happiness.*

KING: "King Solomon." *Prospects for love.* Love and warmth are on the way or may even be present. A man of influence and good intentions interested in the Querent or Subject. An easy going generous masculine influence. *A Protecting individual.*

QUEEN: "The Pink Lady." *The passion card.* It stimulates love situations. It offers joy and pleasure with unqualified love and compassion.. This is action through instinct, not reason. It is friendly and helpful. assistance. *A possible love affair in the future.*

JACK: "The Priest." *A sign of good times and good company.* Loving friends and general good fortune. A carefree interlude with the influence of a confidant. The person with whom one may be involved. *A love affair.* Ten "Castles in Spain". *The wish fulfillment.* The sign of a successful future. A very fortunate romantic card. It is complete fulfillment in an emotional situation. it is triumph against all odds and good luck to any project. It is good news and the reason. to be optimistic. *This is happiness and love.*

NINE: "The Great Nine." *The card of protection.* Spiritual joy in life, with inspirational awareness. It is protection. with the retrieval of losses suffered. There is spiritual well being and inner growth. An alliance with positive life forces is indicated. It is reason for much happiness as there is a positive answer. *This is the wish card.*

EIGHT: "The Party Card." *The card of enthusiasm and gusto.* Friendly reactions from those in the environment. Love and sex are synonymous. Money through love, or a gift which causes pleasure (not necessarily material). It is the formation of friendships with pleasant dispositions. It is the making of the best adjustments. *Good health.*

SEVEN: "Lovers Quarrel." *It concerns romance within the partnership.* A bad omen for marriage. There is an indication of unreliability. Others involved may be apt to change their minds. There is a call for wisdom and reflection to bring calm and serenity to one's surroundings. In that way one can win out over an unpleasant situation. *Love life not stable.*

SIX: "Grace's Card." *Troubles and problems.* An omen of conniving associates. Plans take shape, but others may steal the advantage. It is a sign of emotional disturbances. There is a risk of total failure. No sign of immediate gains or any accomplishment. There seems to be disappointment. *Partial fulfillment of desires.*

FIVE: "Learning of the Truth." *An omen of indecision.* The desire to escape issues. There are regrets, tears and disappointments. Sorrow, however, does not lie deep. An indication of a delightful passing romantic involvement, but not lasting. *There is relief from self imposed bondage.*

FOUR: "The Old Maid." *The sign of stability.* A happy productive and pleasant home life. Happiness through. work and its opportunities. Enrichment of life through service. The stable plan for fulfillment in courtships, engagements and friendships. *Satisfaction where unselfishness is rewarded.*

THREE: "The Lady." *The promise Of increased happiness.* All depends on the Querent's determination. A good idea or heartwarming news. There is fun and friendships and things that are emotionally pleasing. *A happy mental state.*

TWO: "The Falling Star." *The lucky omen of fate and destiny.* The success card. Unexpected good which keeps things moving. (Time Element - 2 days, weeks, months).

SUIT OF DIAMONDS

ACE: "The Pot of Gold." *The constructive power.* Sudden news of a lucky nature. Important information concerning business or money matters. An expansive financial endeavor. Good payment for past efforts. *Good luck.*

KING: "King Midas." *The creator or driving force.* Reward, recognition and dignity for services rendered. The dignified male. A good reputation and long standing situations. (Could be legal Counsel.) A dangerous man, ruthless competitor or rival. Bad or deceitful lover. *Better financial gains*

QUEEN: "Queen Victoria." *The creatve force.* An opportunity to expand the existing circumstances, or to create new ones. Devise for making money. Tremendous potential on both the material and spiritual planes. The flirtatious woman. An unfriendly situation, possibly scandals. Watch out for trickery. (Time Element - 3 days, weeks, months.) *Progress is made.*

JACK: "The Crossroads of Life." *Improved business conditions.* Gains and profit through friendships. The personality is improved. A self centered person. Bad. *Prestigeous luck.*

TEN: "Fortune's Favor." *The sign of wider horizons.* Escape from narrow confining situations in life. Enjoyment of new experiences. A very good card, success, security and freedom from financial fear. *An omen of tremendous gains.*

NINE: "The Curse of Scotland." *The sign of a new start.* Expanded interests. Self improvement, both material and spiritual. Business profit and protected interests. A new undertaking will succeed with satisfaction and happiness. *Secure holdings.*

EIGHT: "Fortress on a Hill." *The sign of balance.* Opportunities at work behind the scenes. Gains are slow but steady in financial matters. Savings grow. Skill, coupled with spiritual, strength. *One is dealt with. fairly.*

SEVEN: "Dispute." *An omen of distress.* The card of bad aspects. Other people's interests take precedence. An unresolved problem involving finances. Do not gamble. There is bad luck in any enterprise or purpose. *A delayed decision.*

SIX: "A Windfall." *Opportunites bringing gain.* Expansion in work situations and increasing income. A warning against an over reliance on material things. *Accept the good with a little caution.*

FIVE: "Napoleon." *The destiny card.* Things beyond one's control come into play. It may be good or bad according to placement, but usually denotes support from the forces of destiny. There may be a. clash of wills over a business matter. Uncertainty in matters of gambling. *An expansion card.*

FOUR: "The Idealist.". *The insurance card.* There is positive outcome in matters of idealism and wisdom. There is a concrete and measurable improvement and success in the financial concerns. Possible quarrels among friends or relatives. *Beware a betrayal of faith.*

THREE: "Thumbs Down." *Omen of the negative answer.* Stop and think all situations over. The sign of separation. There could be a dispute over finances or an entanglement with a negative outcome. (The following cards will indicate the result.)

TWO: Dynamite." *The wild card.* It blasts old patterns in order to create new. There may be an unexpected offer of money or a business venture *A steady increase.*

SUIT OF CLUBS

ACE: "Hammer of Thor." *The power card.* The card of talent and helpful associates. High hopes and ambitions. Ideas and inspirations. Inventive or innovative changes to attitudes. There is strong energy and imagination coupled with power and emotional strength. An important message concerning the initiation of a new venture. *Good luck, financial success and good health.*

KING: "The Crusader." *Overcoming obstacles.* Good advice and help. News about honors and authority. Recognition that is due the Querent. Strength, knowledge and experience. Faithful friendships. *The power of the moral establishment.*

QUEEN: "Lady of the Manor." *A struggle between: desires and obligations.* Difference between needs and wants. An indication of news and many changes. *There is a responsibility to the past.*

JACK: "Edward, the Black Prince." *Things initiated and sustained.* One must be alert. There are changes involving associates and enthusiastic friendships. An aggressive go getter type. Look into all deals. *Keep in control.*

TEN: "Something in the Wind." *A fresh outlook on life.* A new opportunity. Adapting to new ideas. Successful ventures of all kinds. One gets what one wants out of any situation, either pleasure or pain. It wards off the evil of other influences in the cards. *Strong good luck.*

NINE: "The Trouble Card." *A suprise twist to whatever is going on.* Much talk and little action. One may lose some friends because of one's success. Ambition injured by obstinacy. Unexpected opportunity leads to well-being. *Hard work is neccessary.*

EIGHT: "The Glorious Victory." *A fortunate omen denoting harmony.*

Loyal support from those in the environment. It shows a need to communicate in order to reach any agreement. The sign of balance, harmony and spiritual quietude. Inner qualities guard against life's vicissitudes. Caution is urged in money matters. *Happiness increases with time.*

SEVEN: "Lords of Karma." *That which is due one in life.* Much social activity and opportunities for meeting new persons. Business changes for the better (unless coupled with Spades). It shows a need to take time to relax. There may have been arguments or weaknesses that need correcting. Finish what has been started. Money is coming. The repayment of a debt. A warning against an unstable effort and an illusionary success. *An increase in value is indicated.*

SIX: "Unfavorable Partnership." *An energy loss.* That which affects the physical co-operation of efforts. Changes in work situations. Wasted energy and losses. A reaction to a poor attitude. Opportunities for a favorable social life. Changes of attitudes and outlook for the better. *Try harder.*

FIVE: "In the Pits." *End of a cycle.* The situation is hopeless and reaches its conclusion. Nothing more can be gained. Possibility of a quarrel among friends. Rivalry, strife or competition and jealousy. A sign that one needs to take matters in hand and become more self-sufficient. *Move on to other things.*

FOUR: "The Devil's Bedposts." *Increased activities.* A strengthening of friendships and social capacities. Unexpected assistance coming. A day by day growth. The possibility of lies. One is blind to the situation. Self-deception. Sudden misfortune and failure of a project. *The thorn rose.*

THREE: "The Four Leaved Clover." *Omen of good luck.* An activity which has the potential of successful growth. Cleverness and ingenuity. Short comings not recognized. Face facts, make amends. *The idea card.*

TWO: "Tug of War." *The omen of direct opposition.* Associates may oppose one's works. Tremendous power and intensity of emotion. Social invitations of important consequences. Just enough money to get by on. It takes a lone wolf to beat this card. *Luck only by fate.*

Suit of Spades

ACE: "The Black Hole." *The complete negative.* Expectations of the worst. Worry, fear, anxiety and doubt. Setback and delay. Complications in plans. One may be trapped by circumstances. Few or no alternatives. Indecision and possible financial debts. Bad news (legal or emotional), but there is force, power and strength. *Triumph only after severe obstacles.*

KING: "Kaiser Bill." *Losses in position.* Complications from a legal figure, or one in a superior role. An enemy, dishonest and opportunistic. *Be on guard.*

QUEEN: "The Black Maria." *A warning card.* Hidden deceit could cause sorrow. Underhanded tactics, or deliberate delay. The duties in life. Disturbances, scandal and deception. *The card of treachery.*

JACK: "Black Jack." *Unwelcome news.* An evil omen for lovers. Betrayal and dissatisfaction. All is not what it seems to be. A pretended friend. Misfortune through a love affair. Lack of character in a lover. Misfortune to friends and associates. *Dissatisfaction with the way things are.*

TEN: "Walking in Darkness." *A dark body of water by night, the situation looks black.* Trouble, difficulty and pressure from all sides. Disappointment, delay, anxiety, loneliness and setbacks. There are walls and barriers. An abandonment of long cherished plans. (It blights good cards and strengthens evil ones.) *The good is nullified.*

NINE: "The Fall of Gibralter." *An omen of catastrophe.* These are the swift destructive forces of evil. Changes through unexpected and unpredictable sources. Sorrow and defeat, failure in general. Adversity ahead. Things not going the Querent's way. Disappointments and unfortunate spiritual experiences. Watch and wait. Need to develop a responsible attitude. There may be tidings of death or illness. (9 and 10 of Spades - the Death Combination). *Complete adversity.*

EIGHT: "A Dreadful Storm." *Disillusionment and opposition*

looms ahead. Disappointment in plans and wishes. An unhealthy relationship. Difficulty in self-expression. There is a reinforcement of energy. Drop all plans and make a fresh start. (If surrounded by other spades, it could mean a health problem.) *Thorn in the flesh.*

SEVEN: "Seven. Devils." *A sign of division.* A reversal in plans. An unhappy anxious period of time. Does not indicate expected satisfactions or rewards. An upset over unwanted changes over which one has no control. Sorrows and losses in marriage and partnerships. Partners could be at a serious disadvantage affecting the Querent. Poor judgment in legal affairs. Tricks and intrigues. A change for the worst. With forcefulness of character touchy situations improved with time. *Let all matters ride until the bad cycle rolls by.*

SIX: "The Beleaguered Castle." *The card of stress.* A depletion of energy and a lessening of intensity around any particular situation. The breaking of bonds, the cutting of ties. Obligations with little reward. Much planning with little results leads to discouragements. Decisions are made by others. Dismay over work conditions. *There is anxiety and suspended motion.*

FIVE: "Pressures." *Making a voluntary change.* Heavy responsibility with grief, sorrow and remorse. Unfortunate in love matters. Success only after much work and many reverses. *Evaluate all aspects.*

FOUR: "Upward Climb." *A pause to renew strength.* There is a recuperation and healing. There is an end to anxiety and strife. A period of minor aggravation. *Temporary reverses.*

THREE: "The Black Trinity." *Interference.* Trouble in the home. Poor rewards for work done. Mistakes slow down progress. An unhealthy mental attitude. Little solution to problems. *Endure and await a better time.*

TWO: "Either/or." *The wild card of ambivalence.* A stumbling block. Abrupt changes in direction. Complete change or separation. A negative material worth. *Halt spending.*

Spreads for Readings

The Horseshoe Spread – For General Readings

Use a deck that has two Jokers. Mark one for a female Querent and one to represent a male Querent.

Set the Joker as a significator to represent the Querent in the center of the table.

The Reader should shuffle the deck thoroughly and fan it out upon the table. The Querent must then select nine cards from the fan and hand them face down to the Reader. The fan should then be gathered up and set aside.

The Reader then deals out the nine selected cards in a horseshoe shape around the significator starting at the left.

The first three are read as the Past, the second three as the Present and the third as the future, thus:

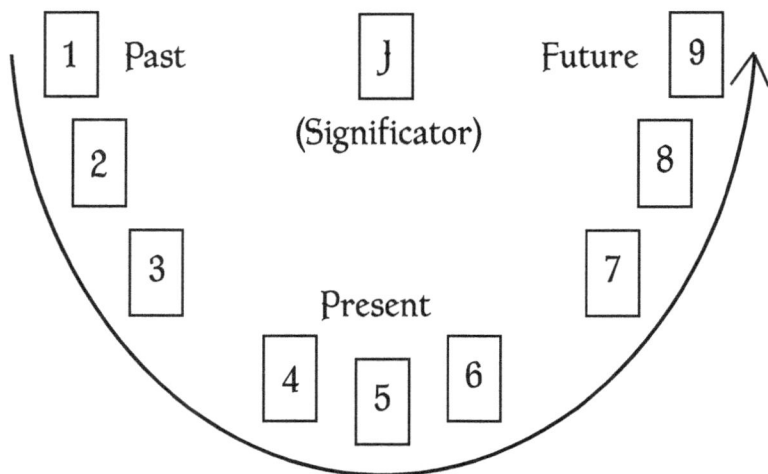

The Horseshoe Spread -- For Specific Questions

The Querent must shuffle and cut the cards. into three piles to the left with the left hand as he or she concentrates on a question needing a specific answer.

The Reader picks up the three piles from the left and deals off seven cards in a horseshoe moving to the left. They are read thus:

1. Past Influences.
2. Present Circumstances..
3. General Future Conditions.
4. Best Course of Action.
5. Attitudes From Others in the Environment.
6. Opposition and Obstacles.
7. Probable Final Outcome.

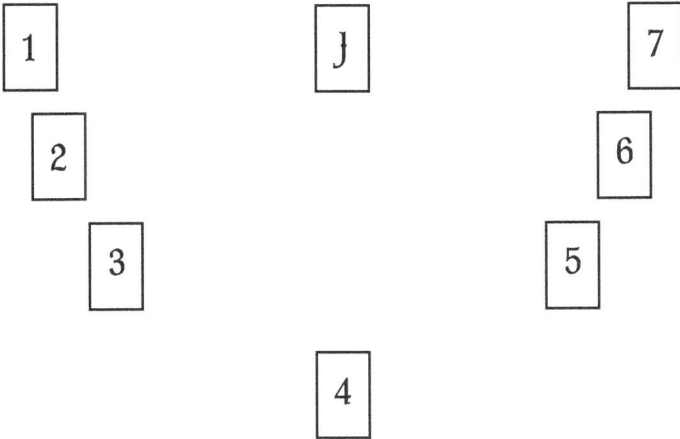

```
  [1]          [J]          [7]

     [2]               [6]

        [3]         [5]

            [4]
```

The Seven Card Advice Spread

Have the Querent shuffle and concentrate on his/her problem or concern. (A Joker should already be set as a Significator.) Lay out the cards from the top of the deck:

1 should be read as the events leading to the Present.
2 & 3 are the cards of the most likely outcome.
4 & 5 are the counsel the Oracle offers.
6 & 7 are the cards for the best course of action to take.

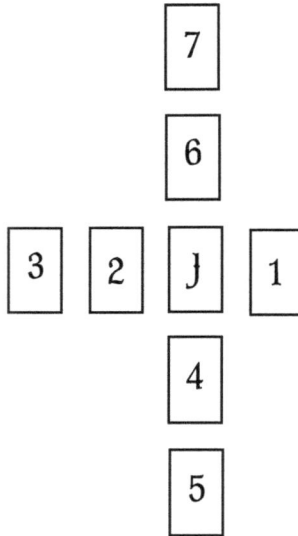

```
          +---+
          | 7 |
          +---+

          +---+
          | 6 |
          +---+

+---+ +---+ +---+ +---+
| 3 | | 2 | | J | | 1 |
+---+ +---+ +---+ +---+

          +---+
          | 4 |
          +---+

          +---+
          | 5 |
          +---+
```

Spread For a Comprehensive Answer
To a Very Heavy Question

The Querent should shuffle the cards very well and deeply concentrate on the matter needing a prognostication.

The cards are not cut, but stacked and handed back to the Reader and dealt from the top.

They are laid in the following sequence and read thus:

Card # 1 & 2 are read as the immediate influences around the matter.
Card # 3 & 4 are the forces coining to bear on the situation.
Card # 5, 6, 7, & 8 are the forces in favor of the Querent.
Card # 9, 10, 11, & 12 are the forces of the opposition.
Card # 13 & 14 are the end results portended.

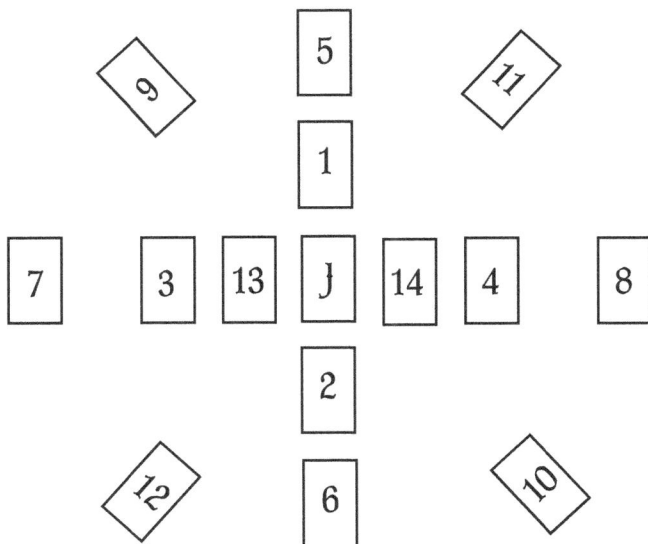

The Seven Sisters – For a Comprehensive Reading

The Querent shuffles the deck and cuts them into three piles to the left with the left hand.

The Reader draws one card off each pile left to right forming a cluster of three cards. This process is repeated six more times, resulting in seven clusters of three, or 21 cards.

The Reader turns each cluster face up and reads left to right The center card in each cluster is the most important, with those on either side qualifying it thus:

Step 1: Querent shuffles and lays cards in 3 piles

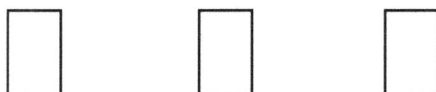

Step 2: Reader draws cards ——›

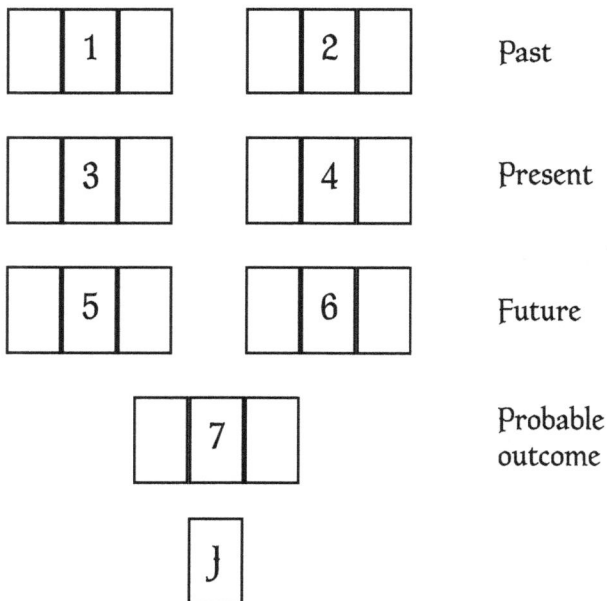

1	2	Past
3	4	Present
5	6	Future
	7	Probable outcome
	J	

Tirage en Croix
(From the French)

The Querent shuffles and cuts the cards into three piles.

The Reader picks up the piles in direct order of the cut, that is, the Querent's first pile ends up on top in the Reader's hands.

Deal out four cards in order three times around using 12 cards in all, or four stacks of three.

Read them thus according to meaning:

Stack # 1 Pertaining to the Self.
Stack # 2 The foundation of the matter.
Stack # 3 The outer world influences.
Stack # 4 The results/La suprise of the Reading.

This gives a general outlook for a Querent's situation.

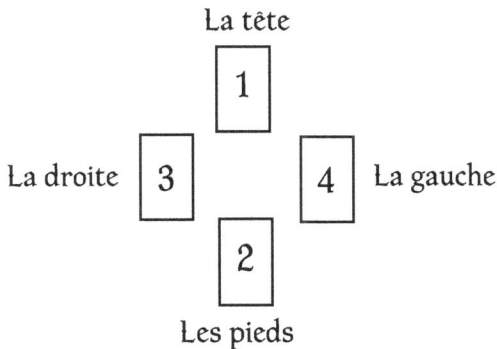

La tête

		1		
La droite	3		4	La gauche
		2		

Les pieds

The Three Card "Yes or No" Spread
For a Quick Answer to a Simple Question

Shuffle the cards well and cut into three piles to the left as the question is concentrated upon. Turn over the piles.

The cards on top are then read thus:

2 red means yes.
2 black means no.
3 red is a positive yes.
3 black is an emphatic no.

III Spirit Runes

	The Windmill: Place this Rune over a doorpost to impede evil and protect property from envy. Inscribe it on a Day of Mercury as Luna wanes. A protective influence around the question, not reversible.
	The Arrow of the Dawn: This Rune symbolizes the Will to Success. Reversed, it stands for Failure. A very positive omen in upright position. It deals with the activities of life and one's affect on others.
	The Spiral of Life, Order, Cosmos. This Rune stands for creative motion. Reversed, it means the Ceasing of Effort. The Karma, or the course of life is proceeding as it should and one's efforts are blessed.
	The Tempest. This Rune represents the forces of strife and chaos. In its reversed meaning, it stands for the containment of strife, or peace. There are wild and contentious forces at work. Seek to control the emotions, or chaos will result.
	The Rain God. This Rune is called the Winds of Change. It causes a movement in circumstances. Reversed, it is the force that resists change. Opportunities and benefit on the way, if upright. Otherwise, the status quo remains the same.
	The Wizard's Bane. This Rune invokes the Air Element to lift any curse or ban. Reversed, it lays one upon a person. Enemies afoot behind the scenes, if reversed. Upright, the forces are removing obstacles.
	The Upliftment. This Rune stands for the indomitable spirit in Man.. Reversed, it means submission to contrary forces. One may overcome any adversity along the path of progress.

	The Flame of Life. This Rune symbolizes spiritual expansion. It is a Blessing Rune and has no reversed meaning. The Light of Heaven shines in the Querent's life and good things are on the way.
	The Trident of Fire. This is a Rune for offence, it means Magical Attack. Reversed, it stands for surrender to such powers. An omen to take the offensive in any situation where action is needed. Reversed, nothing can be done, someone else has the advantage.
	The God's Bolt. In this Rune is the motion of the Life Force. It means courage and power. Reversed, it is the destructive use and results of power. A way will be knocked through any blocks. Reversed, no victory in the long run.
	The Goddess's flame. This Rune stands for spiritual. protection and the tranquil hearthfire. It is a Blessing Rune and may not be reversed. The positive sign of happy and contented home life.
	The Eye of Wrath. This Rune represents anger and rage. Reversed, it is the Star of Harmony and used to calm tempers. The destructive is allowed the upper hand and only ruin will result.
	The Sea. This Rune symbolizes the churning of emotional situations. Reversed, it is called Oil on the Waters, and stands for calmness. Relationships are not clear, but cloudy and uncertain. Not evil, but a caution in love is indicated.
	The Chalice. For happy containment in love and all that love would represent. Reversed, it is The Spilling Out and means the loss of love. The perfect match for love. A very good omen for affairs of the heart.
	The Wave. This Rune stands for the Force of Life in full flow. Its reversed meaning is The Abyss which has no way out. All is happening as it should to the best advantage possible. A mature outlook to the situation.

	The Blessed. This Rune means emotional stability and life in perfect balance. It can not be reversed.. Health and wellbeing is indicated. A good omen of right thinking and doing,
	The Hood. This Rune represents heightened psychic awareness. When reversed, it is the Barb, or evil magics. Sensitivity to life is good. The inner being is progressing well. Reversed, adverse psychic forces at work.
	The Flower. This Rune is the fruit of Maturity and Wisdom. Reversed, it is the Fall, or instability. One's plans coming to fruit as planned. This is the right course to follow. In an ill aspect, the insecure is causing pressures and changes, not for the good.
	The Barrier. This Rune impedes progress and may be used both for offense and defense. The definite NO! Abandon all hope. Nothing will come of this question or course of action.
	The Tree. This Rune stands for life, growth and nourishment. In a reversed position, it is the Spearhead and means death. Upright, the YES and the way to go.
	The Platter And Loaf. The meaning of this Rune is prosperity and abundance. Reversed, it is the Bare Table and brings hunger and want. Money. The sign of positive material worth.
	The Far Horizon. This Rune offers power and dominion. Reversed, it is the Sun Below, and means the loss of property. The positive indication of advancement and opportunity in expanding one's horizons. Better relations on the job and with associates.
	The Shield. This Rune stands for the powers of defense. Reversed, it means the depths of defeat. A time to be on guard and prepared for any eventuality. Upright, one will win out. Reversed, the power rests in other hands.

Cycles. In an upright position, it represents good over evil. When reversed, it is the triumph of evil. The matter has run its course and the results are as they are. Reversed, only a bitter harvest is due.

The Spirit Runes are not of the ancient lore of Wizardry, but are of this Day and Age. They came from meditation on the Mercurial Power and offer a minor form of Divination such as the Playing cards.

They are not a deep oracle, but give a prognostication into the mundane questions affecting the Human Animal.

As a Witch, people will come to you and ask your insight into their problems and want to know what they should do.

By casting these runes you will be able to get a general insight into their situations and be able to offer an answer.

On a Day of Mercury, as the Moon waxes in a Water Sign, go out into Nature under Wind and Sky and search for 24 flat round pebbles of about two inches across.

Paint them white and inscribe the runes on them on one side only in black paint. The backs of the pebbles should be white, but unadorned.

At night on that Day of Mercury, pass them eight times through the smoke of a Mercurial Incense and repeat eight times over them:

Runes of seeing, Runes of rede,
give the answer one must heed.
What be the doom that we must deem?
Omens of luck, or a Night Hag's scream?
Runes of gladness, Runes of woe,
show us true the way to go.

Then place the runes stones in a small box and put them away for future use.

How to Cast The Spirit Runes

Make for yourself a Rune Cloth of dark blue. It should be no more than one square yard of material, a natural linen, or cotton, or leather or skin would be favored above any synthetic fabric.

You may adorn the cloth either with embroidery or fine paint with any symbols desired that reflect the idea of the Mercurial power or of the old Norse God Odin. Dark blue was His color.

This cloth you would only use for casting the Runes upon, spread out on a table or flat surface. They may also be kept wrapped in the Rune Cloth when not in use.

Cast Runes on a Night of Mercury when He be not Retrograde, but moving direct and best if Luna passes in an Air Sign and waxes.

In that way Rune Casting would be done in the time and favorable influences conducive thereto.

Burn an Incense of Mugwort and Mace which favor the Psychic Powers at such times.

The Spirit Runes are to be read for yourself alone and not in the company of others. You may, however, read that which would pertain to others in consulting the Runes.

Cast the Magic Circle and stand to face East across thy Altar and have the Rune Cloth laid out upon it before you.

Holding the Rune stones in both hands cupped together, pass them eight times through the smoke of the Incense and say:

Hermes, Thoth and Odin art thou known among mankind.
Attend to me in this great need.
Thy wisdom and elucidation I would have.
Lead me to the light out of dark unknown.

Holding the Runes close to your breast, meditate deeply on that question or matter for which you seek an answer for about 8 minutes quietly and intently.

Let the Incense fill the Chamber.

When you feel ready, cast the 24 stones forth onto the cloth and let them fall where and as they may.

You should remove to the side those which fall face down.

Read only those which fall face up from the furthest point from you, moving back toward yourself. The last and closest Rune should be the answer and the others contributory thereto.

Ponder the doom and deem it well. All the Runes pertain to the final one and create the answer you seek.

You can then ask as many questions as needed, but cast them in like manner one question at a time during the course of the night. However, not more than eight castings should be done in one session.

Record your results in your journal and close the Magic Circle and clear all away.

By keeping the Spirit Runes as a personal Oracle for yourself conducted in a ritual manner thus, they become highly charged and attuned only to your employ in the Mercurial works.

You should, at all times, keep them from being handled by any other person, no matter how close.

Should they be handled by others, they must then be re-consecrated in like manner, as indicated above.

———————⊰❈⊱———————

Scrying in The Goddess's Name

On Nights of Luna as She waxes in Water Signs, set two violet, blue or white candles to burn beside a Chalice of water. Allow a fragrant Incense such as Jasmine or Sandalwood to lightly scent your Ritual Chamber.

Sit yourself comfortably at a table with the candles and Chalice set before you.

Gather the Coven[1] all around to concentrate and invoke the Lunar Orb from on high.

All in unison then must chant:

Come down, come down
in thy gossamer gown.
Into our circle place thy crown.
Give us thy mystery in water by vision
and knowledge to know its meaning by precision.
Come, O Goddess of the Tide of Life,
bring peace and love and an end to strife.
Come down! come down,
O Lady of renown!
Bring thy smile, belie the frown.
What is thy will? What redes dost thou bring?
Inspire us as we chant and sing.
Witches call thee this night of Luna,
Mater Dea, Bona Fortuna!
Come down! Come down, O Mistress of Night,
answer our plea! Allay our plight!

The Witch then goes into light trance to scry in the reflections dancing on the surface of the water.

He/She speaks out what is given to see. The Seer may be questioned

---

1) Author's note: For a Coven rite, an Artisan II° could be the Seer, or the High Priestess or a Hand Maiden/Practicus III°. However, this may be better suited for the Coven women to perform.

and asked to answer what the visions in the water would say to individuals in the Coven Group.

It would be a violation of Witch Law not to give the contents of a vision thus conjured, be it good or ill. The Goddess will speak as She will.

When the conjured vision begins to fade, or when it is felt the power starting to wane, the Seer blows out the candles and says:

Blessed Lady of the Sky,
bless us before thou doth
upward fly. We thank thee
for thy visions so keen.
We know what to do, we
have seen. Blessed be!

The results of such vision rites should be entered into the Coven's Log.

SCRYING IN THE GOD'S NAME

(Author's Note: The same format, as above, can be done with this rite as to the person acting as Seer. But, perhaps the males in the Coven would be better suited.)

On Nights of Mars, as the Moon waxes in a Fire Sign, have procured a tag lock from the person about whom you would know.

Pour a small amount of alcohol (Isopropol) into a metal container of either brass, iron or steel.

Gather the Coven around to link up with the God by this collective chant:

Mars, the warrior, God of Fire!
Heed our call, answer our desire.
Beat the drums and thunder thy roar.
We seek to know what doth go on before.
Come, O tramper and marcher of power!
We call thee in thy rulerships hour.
Burn, burn, the flames mount high!

Come cracking and thundering out of the sky!

As the alcohol is set ablaze, these words are said:

We call thee in thy blazing fire most bright.
Illumine our minds, O God of Light!

The Seer holds the tag lock to the brow or Solar Plexus and concentrates on the individual from whom it came as he/she gazes into the fire and goes into light trance.

Soon visions will be seen in the dancing flames as he/she scrys.

One must then speak out what is seen as this reverie proceeds.

Those in the Coven, most concerned with the Subject's welfare, whereabouts, or doings, may pose questions to the Seer which are answered as the fire reveals them.

As with Scrying in the Goddess's Name, when the conjured energy seems to begin to slack off and wane, the Seer will smother over the fire with a black cloth to put it out and say:

Thank thee, thank thee, God of Light.
We bid thee return to thy orbit in flight.
Pax tibi, pax tibi, pax tibi this night.

THE CRONE'S BLESSING

As part of the presentation of a Wiccan Born at the Covenstead (see *Book II* of *The Sacred Pentagraph*) this minor rite may be performed.

The oldest woman of the Coven would bestow this Witches Blessing on the Newborn.

For a male child she would use Air and Fire, that is Incense and a candle. The Incense would be of Frankincense and a white candle would be lit from the Coven's Sacred Flame.

She would circumambulate the infant boy thrice widdershins as she invokes the Gods thus:

Lord and Lady of our Ancient Faith,
bless this manchild and keep him in thy light.
Powers of the God bless this infant by Air and Fire.
Give him strength and manly grace.
Keep him in the wisdom ways of the Old Gods.
Let not the circle be broken,
that the future be assured.
Blessed be, (infant's name), and blessed be!

For the female child, she would circumambulate with a Chalice of Water and a plate of salt with a small piece of bread or cake. These words are spoken:

Lady and Lord of Witchery and Lore, keep this womanchild
forevermore. Bless her with thy mysterious power, to blossom
as a rose of love.
Powers of the Goddess of Life, bless by water, Earth and love.
Keep her in the Lady's ways all the remainder of her days.
Blessed be, (infant's name), and blessed be!

The Crone, at the last line of each blessing, whispers the secret, magical name into the infant's ear, so only the babe could hear it. The name would be indicative of the powers personified by the child either chosen by the parents, or bestowed by the Crone from her own repository of Wiccan Lore.

From that day forward, no one, absolutely no one, will speak that name, nor allow anyone to ever know it.

The Crone and/or the Parents will take that name to their graves so the secret will be safe.

From that time on, no form of adverse Occult Powers could affect the child on through adulthood, not ever having the real secret name.

In Memoriam

Part of the Women's Mysteries in a Coven is to mark the passing of life from this Earth Plane.

High Priestesses, or the women acting as their delegates, would observe a novena in honor of a deceased Covener 30, 60 and 90 days after his/her passing.

It can be done either with Seven Day glass candles burning for 90 days, or a large white candle could be set to burn itself out for the 30th, 60th and 90th day after the passing.

The candle need not be dressed with any oil, nor would any incense be necessary.

We know persons pass on to bigger and better things. Therefore, Wicca does not Egyptianize the fact of death, nor do we expect to put on the public show of sorrow and mourning, as seen in most other faiths.

We prefer to send love and good will following after the dead. That way, the spiritual essence of the deceased is not held back toward the Earth Plane. Mourning can become morbid and affect those who passed in an adverse way.

On the 30th day after a Covener has crossed the veil, the High Priestess will set the candle alight and say:

God and Goddess of our Ancient Faith,
we commit to thee the spirit of _____,
Brother/Sister of this Coven.
Now we set the Memorial Light
to keep the ways of Ancient Rite.
See this candle burning bright,
to speed this soul beyond the night.
Upward and onward to spiritual progression
says our ancient mode of confession.
Never to stop nor make digression,
Universes unfold without retrogression.
Leave the flesh and take to wing

as joyous and blessed thy voice doth sing.
Love and fellowship is the only thing
that the cycles of time around will bring.
_____, may the Lord and Lady receive thee.
As things unfold, as is the plan, mayest thou once
more find a loving Wiccan hearthfire as
thou returnest in a more perfected state
of being. Blessed be and blessed be!

The same is repeated on the 60th and 90th day after the Covener's passing. Ever afterwards is that Covener only spoken of with fond thoughts. Only to be remembered at his/her best.

Such is the Wiccan attitude to death.

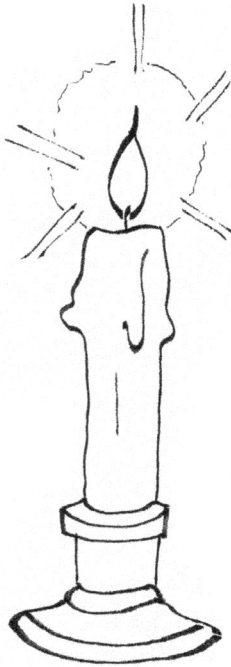

CRAFT POPPETRY FOR THE WITCH

The use of Poppets has been an ancient art passed down in the Craft from distant times.

Poppetry operates on the assumption of a Law of Sympathetic Contagion, where an item from a person, or intimately in association with him/her, is acted upon magically, to produce an affect physically and/or astrally upon the person.

The item from the subject/victim may be hair, nail clippings, body fluids or worn garments. It would be termed in the old idiom a Tag Lock. It is somehow woven into the structure of the Poppet to help identify the Poppet, in the Practitioner's mind, as the subject/victim.

The Tag Lock, being a natural substance, would contain the essence of the person from whom it came; his/her astral counterpart, so to speak. What would be done to it, theoretically, would be done to the person. (If pieces of garment are used, be sure they are natural fibers and not of a synthetic substance, as is common in materials for dress in this day.)

The body of the Poppet could be cut out of felt or flannel, or better yet, from a garment of the subject/victim. (However poppets can be obtained, the usual store bought variety is common. Red or black would be the traditional colors for the Poppet.)

Cut out two sides from a doll pattern and sew them together. Leave a small opening in one foot to place in the stuffing and the Tag Lock.

The stuffing should be herbs associated with the reason for the spell in which the Poppet is employed:

Mint, Lavender, Verbena or Rose Petals for works of love.
Sunflower Petals, Marigold Buds and Hyssop for healing.
Dill Seed, Five Finger Grass, Basil or Cinnamon for Luck and Money matters.
Patchouli, Valerian, Mugwort and Mullein for the works of hexerei.

Once stuffed and with the Tag Lock worked in, the last bit of stitching can be completed to finish the Poppet.

It would be best within the Magical Tradition to make the Poppet in a properly cast Magic Circle. Use either the Circle of Initiates from *Book II* of *The Sacred Pentagraph*, or the simple Circle described in this volume earlier on.

Have all necessary items for making the Poppet and for the spell in which it is to be used on the Altar at the appropriate Planetary Day or Night.

Fridays for Love. Wednesdays for Luck/Money. Sundays for Healing, or Saturdays for Binding and Thwarting. Tuesdays for Blasting enemies. Keep to the suggestions as to the phases of the Moon, etc., as already explained.

Cast the Circle, according to the prescribed ritual and then begin to construct the Poppet.

As it is being made, hold vividly in mind the subject/victim and the purpose for the spell.

With each stitch of the sewing needle, chant a ditty to embody the idea, or the reason for the Poppet:

Stick and sew, stick and sew, by the works of stitchery,
I work my Magic Witchery.
Sew and stick, sew and stick, this little poppet doll
becomes the one whose name I call.
By needle and thimble,
with fingers so nimble,
for spells of (purpose), from long ago,
I employ the Witchy Art I know!

Then the Poppet must be identified as the subject/victim by a process of repeating the person's name over it at least three times, using warm breath if the spell is of a beneficial nature and a cold one, if for a negative purpose, by blowing and whispering the name over the poppet thrice:

Little doll, thou art now known
as the one whose name be blown
over and upon thee yet.
Thou art (name), (name), (name),
thou canst bet!

From this point proceed to work whatever spell would be necessary, such as driving a pin into the region of the heart activating love; binding the doll's arms and limbs to prevent or thwart action, impede physical function; sewing up the mouth to stop talk, or by using a pin to place in a spot needing healing; etc., etc.

For whatever reason the Poppet is being used, the emotion for the spell must be felt and experienced as real; love-hate-compassion, etc.

The chants embodying the idea should be from the Practitioner's own composition, as he/she is more personally involved with the case at hand.

It should be a vivid ritual drama to recreate, as clearly as possible, the reason for the spell. The Poppet is emoted over until a point of emotional exhaustion is reached.

Then the Circle is closed.

Repeat the Spell as often as may be necessary to accomplish the task and then dispose of the Poppet in the way appropriate to the purpose of the working.

Craft
Poppetry

NECROMANCY DIVINATION BY SHADES OF THE DEAD

At the waning of the Moon, in the dark days after the Winter Solstice, when the Sun be in the Sign of the Goat Fish and all sleepeth the great Death at the waning of the year, thou canst summon and question shades . . . .

Necromancy is the Art of communicating with and obtaining information from the Shades of the Departed. It is almost a forgotten form in this modern World.

However, Necromancy has always been a part of any decent Wizard's repertoire, and to do it effectively, serious thought and study must be undertaken.

There are several forms of Necromancy still being used today. One is the Dumb Supper performed by certain Covens of Witches on the Night of Hallowmas, the other form, most commonly heard of, is the seance, held by a Spiritual Medium.

The Medium may think and feel he/she is in actual contact with a sort of "Spirit Guide" which helps bring in the other Shades to be questioned by the sitters in the circle.

True spiritualistic phenomena brings through the actual personality of the deceased individual for all to hear and recognize.

I will give two forms of Necromancy for the Witch and allow him/her to attune the self to the one most suitable to his/her own nature.

It may be good for the Witch to set up his/her own seance group and communicate with the Shades of the Departed who wish to speak to the living, on this side of the veil.

The deeper one gets into this type of phenomena, the more one will see there is really a thin line between the two, and that they on the other side, are not much different than those on this.

First, some pointers to avoid:

Do not use a totally black room. Do not use black cloths on the table. Do not use any heavy incenses.

In a spiritualistic circle, one is opening up to the influences from the other realms. The Dark ones must be left where they are.

Most Spirits are no different than the general run of people. There are good, bad and in between. Leave the criminal element in its own milieu.

It is best to always sit on the same day of the Week, best on Wednesday Nights, at about the same hour each week.

Use a dim room, painted a pale white. Use a white cloth on the table. Use a light fragrant Incense and have flowers on the table and a bowl of water in the center (the flowers could float in the water) to absorb any hostile psychic influences. Flowers give an essence.

Ring the bowl of water with a circle of 8 white candles, which should be the only illumination for the seance.

Have the above arranged and the candles lit along with the Incense at least five minutes before the "Sitting" is to begin.

The Sitting should be composed of a few serious-minded friends or associates, or Coven members, who are interested in Psychic Studies and are agreeable to sitting and developing a Spirit Circle.

They must be knowledgeable enough to know it may take weeks or even months of constant weekly sitting before a clear channel can be established and open to the other side.

For the first several sessions nothing at all may happen. The spirits must be convinced of your sincerity and perseverance before they may wish to attend.

Be skeptical of immediate results. It may be a trickster on either side of the veil.

The number of people should be as even as possible between males and females. They should sit alternating male, female around the table to keep a balance.

With a serious frame of mind, meet each week and allow the group to simply sit around the table and meditate on seeking a rapport with those in Spirit. No specific individuals should be called at the beginning.

After about a half hour, have the group, break the meditation and discuss what was experienced in the session. Have a member act as recorder and keep a journal of the results of each and every meeting.

With time, a channel will open to the other side. Impressions will come through and certain individuals in the group will feel strongly that they must voice them.

Mediums who rock back and forth, gasp and moan and thrash

around are a product of Hollywood movies, and not the norm.

However, with serious cultivation., one in the group may develop into a good sensitive.

Then trance phenomena may manifest.

Do not touch the entranced Medium while it lasts, until the spirit has finished speaking and departs.

You will know the phenomena is real when you afterwards stroke the medium's arms upward to restore circulation. He/she will feel cold to the touch.

Once a channel has been opened, regular sessions will bring through much information.

A "Spirit Guide" may be the main contact with the other side. Do not believe all the mystical hogwash about Spirit Guides some people tell you.

They are not the Mystic Masters of lost Atlantis. They are not great Priests or Priestesses from the Temples of Ancient Egypt. They are not Mahatmas and Gurus of Hindu lore.

They are not Amerindian Shamans. And certainly not Amy Semple McPhearsen.

They are the collective over-soul of the group, itself.

Do not let the overly credulous and the deliberate phonies waste your time and sap your energy.

The Spirit Guide will manifest with each and every session, once serious practice has opened a channel. .

Then, after a considerable amount of experience has been gained by the group as a whole, specific Spirits may be contacted and asked to speak through the group or its Medium.

This form of Necromancy does not constrain or conjure the Spirit against its Will. The over-soul of the group establishes a rapport with the Spirit and invites it to manifest.

Begin by contacting Spirits of people known to someone in the group, so as to have a confirmation of the authenticity of the personality of the being contacted.

When positive results are forthcoming, then "strangers"/non-coveners may be allowed to attend the sessions, so that the group's Spirit Guide may contact those they wish to question.

A reputation for honesty and authentic Spirit Contact will then begin to grow.

A session should begin by having the sitters link hands around the table to keep a closed circuit of living entities and give life to the over-soul of the group.

The meditation should begin and the group sensitives may link up with it.

In the glow of the candles, with water, flowers and light Incense, there is no possibility of phony tricks, as can be done in a totally dark room, so loved by some commercial Mediums.

Keep the hands of all sitters linked through the entire session. That way contact is not lost with the over-soul.

You will have to play much by ear, and allow the group to set its own pace in these matters. I can only give a few hints to help you along.

In questioning the shades of the departed, the matter of foretelling the future usually comes up in the course of time. Do not expect Spirits to reveal the secrets of all the ages to you. They do not know them.

They can, however, see the immediate Astral Influences around individuals, which are about to come into being. No more, no less. They also are fallible, since they were mere Human Beings themselves.

Death, or that state we call such, does not elevate one into the Privy Council of the Most High Gods themselves.

We call such contacts "Spirits." That is really a misnomer for what it is. The Spirit of any departed individual has elevated and gone to its place in the beyond and away from the Earth Plane. Mediumistic Circles can only contact Astral Shells.

Why else do you think I mentioned identifying the "personality" in the explanations above? The shell has a life of its own on the lower planes directly above this one for a period of time after death and maintains its identity and persona, but it is not the real spiritual essence of the departed. It is but a part thereof and a layer of the being that also is cast off, like the body.

The prognostications derived from them, can be useful, but see the Spirits for what they are and do not be mislead by false information.

In this field of the Occult, it is mandatory to keep one's feet on the ground.

Practice Spirit Communication and learn what it can teach, but do not let yourself be carried away.

Concerning the Wizard's
Triangle of Manifestation or
The Seal of Spirits

It should be made new for each ceremony in which such may be called for. The particulars for its making will follow.

It may be drawn in chalk on the Ritual Chamber floor, or made on a large parchment so the smaller parchment containing the Sigil of the individual Spirit to be summoned can be set within it.

The Sigils of individual Spirits or Powers which the Witch would invoke are the symbols associated with the name of the Spirit or Power itself. These can be obtained from many books on Ceremonial Magic readily available, such as *The Grimoire of Armadel*, by Mathers from Weiser, or *The Lesser Key of Solomon*, or *The Arbatel of Magick*.

The idea being, that the "Force" or Power, which is called a Spirit, is meditated upon, invoked and constrained to enter the Triangle of Manifestation to rest, on or above its own Sigil or Symbol. That is done by use of the proper Incense, number vibration, colors and Words of Power to which the old Grimoires say the Spirit will respond. The Witch will, of course, be within the Magic Circle and conjure the Spirit to attend and enter the Triangle.

From there, the Witch will lay or put whatever Charge or request he/she Wills upon the Spirit to bring about his/her Will.

The Medieval Ceremonial Magicians and Wizards called the Powers Spirits, but they are not really what normally today is meant by the word. They are the lesser Forces of the Divine ALL, which have particular responsibilities in the overall scheme of the Cosmos, both for good, or ill, as we see it. They are neither good or evil in themselves.

The process is one of attracting that particular Force and filling it with one's own Will and desires. As long as the Will or desire corresponds to the particular Province of the individual Spirit, the Will of the Wizard/or Witch can be made to come about, according to the old lore.

In times long ago, when Humanity was more primitive in its thinking, blood of animals, and even, Humans, were used to place beside the Symbol or link for attracting the Spirit.

The "Beings" invoked, drew strength from the essences given off by blood.

Today, the same can be accomplished by using a living essence in much the same way, but not blood.

Beside the Sigil in the Triangle, place a small bowl into which a raw egg has been cracked open, or a flower of the color of the Spirit Force may be set in a small vase with water.

When that is combined with the proper Incense, there is sufficient essence given off to allow the Spirit to draw energy and assume a temporary Astral vehicle in the Invocations.

An egg or flower represents the basic forms of life and would be better than blood, which may only attract beings from the Chaos.

(Traditional sources)

TRIANGLE OF MANIFESTATION
SEAL OF SPIRITS

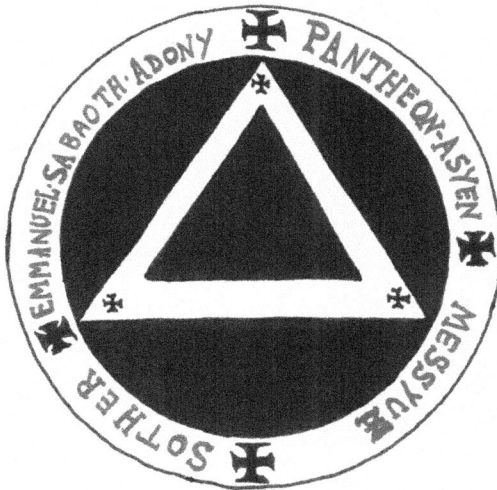

Inscribe this Seal outside your Magic Circle at the Quarter
from whence, you would summon a particular Spirit.

Scribe the Spirit's name along the three sides of the triangle and set the Sigil of the Spirit
scribed on parchment in ink of Dragons-Blood in the, center thereof.

From within your Magic Circle, burning the proper Incense,
and reciting the proper Invocation, you can summon the Spirit to attend the rite and charge it to do your Will.

You can also scribe this Seal on parchment and surround it with three candles of black or white, and place therein a Crystal Ball to scry the portends of Time and Space.

It is into the center of this Seal, that the link would be cast during the Ritual to follow, so that no Sigil would be needed, when the Spirit summoned is a deceased person and not of other orders of being.

The High Ceremony of Necromancy
To Summon Shades of The Departed

(Keeping this ceremony in old idiom, to impress the deep mind.)

Such wouldst thou do only upon great need and in pressing circumstance after much deliberation and deep thought given thereto.

Thou art dealing with the Mysteries from the Beyond and it be a heavy and dire working, dangerous to the unprepared.

In the waning of the year, from the Autumnal Equinox to the Winter Solstice, is the only time thou shouldst attempt to conjure the Shades from the Beyond. The best times would be at the Dark of the Moon on a Night of Saturn as the Sun passeth in the Sign of Capricorn.

However, The Waning Moon Nights of Mercury during the Winter Season from Hallows to Midwinter are also favorable.

That be the Season of Death and the breaking down of Life, preparatory to the deep sleep of Winter. The Spirits are stirring at that time, it is traditionally said, and may be more easily attracted. The veil between life and death is thin at that time.

Thou wouldst not perform this Necromancy in the presence of other living persons, but alone within thy Magic Circle.

Shouldst thou have an apprentice to the Arts of Wizardry or Witchcraft, that thou teacheth and traineth to follow after thee, then he/she may be allowed to sit within thy Circle to observe the Ritual, but not actively participate, nor contribute thereto.

Thy Chamber should be dark and draped in black. Thy Altar cloth and all candles be also of that shade. Thy robe and cord should also be black.

Thy manner and mien shouldst be dark and somber and commanding. Not the forceful commanding manner of a warrior, but the cold, hard, steady approach of one who knoweth dark things. Cold and firm, shouldst be thy bearing. All must be dark and heavy around thee.

Heed well these words of warning and follow them to the letter, or thou place thyself in grave peril. Thou couldst fall into the Abyss of Madness and do great damage to thy sanity and equilibrium, as the Ancient Sages have warned.

Obtain the necessary items and put them together as I instruct thee. Foolhardiness and frivolity wouldst abort the effort.

Decide what information thou require from the Beyond and meditate deeply on it to obtain a clear, precise idea.

Choose the Spirit thou wouldst conjure. It must have been on the other side of the veil for at least a year and a day.

Have at hand a personal item from that Spirit when it was in physical bodily form. That be thy link to the personality thou wouldst conjure.

Obtain Dittany of Crete, Patchouli, Mugwort, Valerian and Black Arts Incense.

Wear a Pentagram of Silver whenever dealing with Spirits, as it is a symbol of mastery in the Occult.

Thou must have the items ready before two weeks prior to the Night chosen for the Ritual.

Two Weeks prior, thou must retire nightly into thy Chamber and light a black candle and hold the link in thy hand. Meditate deeply on the name of the Spirit thou wouldst conjure for about one Quarter of an hour, as thou grind in thy mortar and pestle, the herbs above mentioned and mix them well with the Black Arts Incense.

In other words, nightly, thou must meditate with the link and grind thy mixture picturing the Spirit summoned to thee. Such will open a channel and rapport with the Shade/Spirit so it may more readily be summoned on the Night of the Ritual.

If thou canst not set aside the necessary amount of time, abort thy effort and attempt it not.

On the Night of the Ritual, thy Altar candles must be black, thy four Quarter candles around thy Circle must be black, thy Altar also draped therewith and thy robe and Ritual Chamber also black.

In the center of thy Altar should sit thy Burner and thy Incense mixture.

Thou must face West across the Altar towards the Quarter whence the Winter Sun went down.

Have thy hand bell near thy Incense.

Deep in the night, at the Midnight Hour approach thy Altar and ring the bell 11 times.

Follow thy usual format to cast thy Magic Circle. (Should thy Apprentice be with thee, he/she must sit quietly at the East side within the Circle).

Use some of thy Incense mixture to cast the Circle, and keep a goodly amount handy to use during the Ritual.

Thy manner must be cold and firm. Thy voice commanding and forceful.

When thy Circle be erect and the Ritual ready to proceed, state aloud:

We come in the Dead of Night, in the waning of the year, to summon the forces of the Beyond.
Wardens of the gates, swing open the doorway. Send forth the Spirit of the one I call. . . . . .
I be the servant of the Nameless One! Amen Selah!

Rap thrice upon thy Altar with thy knuckles loudly. (Remember, thou should have placed a Seal of Spirits to the West outside thy Circle bearing the name of the one to be summoned.

Thou must repeat the words above twice more.

Add more Incense to the coals as needed.

Take up thy Sword or Athame and step to the West side of the Circle and point it down toward the Seal of Spirits. Cast the link, the item belonging to the Spirit when it was in this life, upon the Seal.

Speak out:

By thy own do I summon thee! By thine own essence art thou bound to attend upon me!
By thy life, that thou werdst, must thou come!
Conjured and constrained be to do my Will!
I be the servant of the Nameless One! Amen, Selah!

Thou must here pause and allow a silence to ensue. Things may begin to stir outside thy Circle.

Under no circumstances, from this time on, must anything leave thy

Circle.

Thou must have firm command of all that happens from this point.

Return to stand across the Altar facing West to the Seal of Spirits and add more Incense as needed.

Set thy Sword or Athame back in place and take up thy hand bell once again.

Ring the bell 12 times and say:

At the twelve strokes of time, be summoned to obey!

Allow a silence to ensue again and listen for any sound round about thy Circle.

After the slight pause, speak forth the Necromantic Charge:

By the powers of this dying year,
by the waning of the moon,
by the western shores of life,
by the Night of Time and space,
by the words of Will and might
(Name of Spirit), come forth!
By the works of wizardry and wonder,
by the darkness of the grave,
by the force of Gods and man,
by the summons from the dark,
by the scent of herb and smoke
come forth!
By the Dark Angel's bidding,
by the bounds of living essence,
by the Seal of Spirit manifest,
by the command of the Nameless One,
by dark candle's light,
(Name of Spirit), come forth!
Enter into this world of form.
Clothe thyself in smoke.
Approach the Seal of Spirits.
Pantheon Asyen!
Messyuz!
Sother! . . . .

Emmanuel Sabaoth Adonoy!
Be subject unto me!

Thou should add more incense at this time and take the burner and place it at the western rim within thy Circle, near the place of the Seal of Spirits.

A presence will now be felt to manifest outside the Circle near the Seal. Allow it to swirl and form as it will in the Incense. Lift high thy Sword or Athamé to the West and speak:

(Name of Spirit), thou art summoned to answer my questions truly and without delay! Give forth thy answer!

Now thou must put what query thou wilt to the Shade.

It must be the precise wording for the purpose thou meditated upon during the two weeks prior to this Night.

After the question, allow all to go silent and await thy answer. It may not be an audible voice thou hearest, but a deep impression of words and symbols coming to thy mind.

Remember everything which happens in this long silence. Record it later.

After a good few minutes, the atmosphere will begin to grow light as the power begins to wane. That is the sign that the session is over.

Thou may have beheld a form taking shape in the dim light and Incense smoke during the silence. Study it well, but do not disturb it by any sound made from thyself or thy Apprentice whatsoever.

The Shades are very nebulous and are easily dissipated by vibrations.

It will begin to fade of itself when the feeling of the lighter atmosphere ensues.

Allow the energy to drain away by itself. Then thou canst begin to close the Ritual.

Take thy Sword or Athamé to the West Quarter and holding it high, begin to trace a Banishing Pentagram towards the West with these words:

Close the Veil, banish the Power, seal the Gates!
Spirit of (Name of Spirit), return to thy proper place in space and time. Depart this realm of matter and be at peace! Amen, Selah!

Return thy Sword or Athamé to its place on the Altar and take thy hand bell and ring it 13 times and say:

All Shades and lingering Phantoms be gone and away!

Then close thy Circle in the proper fashion.

When all has been done, then and only then shouldst thou step out of the Circle area.

Burn some Frankincense to cleanse away the heaviness and change the vibrations.

Thou canst then record thy impressions.

In the course of the following days and weeks, thy question to the Spirit will bring an answer to thee in mysterious ways. Be ready and open to everything pertaining thereto, and thy works of Necromancy will bring thee positive results.

If nothing seems to transpire during the Ritual, think not that it worketh naught. Not all are sensitive to see or hear Spirit voices. Thou wilt, however, feel the heaviness of the presence of something outside thy Circle.

It would communicate with thee to answer thy question in the way most conducive to thy psychology and understanding.

The Spirit Realm will give thee a response to the question asked in whatever form thou could safely handle.

The ideas pertaining to the Spirits in the use of communicating in a Spirit Circle, in the pages above, would also apply in the ritual approach such as this.

Do not summon the Dead for light or frivolous matters, but question them only for solutions to problems thou canst not deal with thyself.

Remember, their powers of foretelling the future are limited and can only be accurate in the short run.

(Author's note: The divine names used in the Necromantic Charge are from traditional ceremonial ritual procedures.)

TALISMANS OF THE CORNUCOPIA

These minor Talismans for the Planetary Influences are offered in this Book as an example of Magical Procedure and methods of Consecration.

The Covener may use them in his/her Ordeal to attain Artisan status.

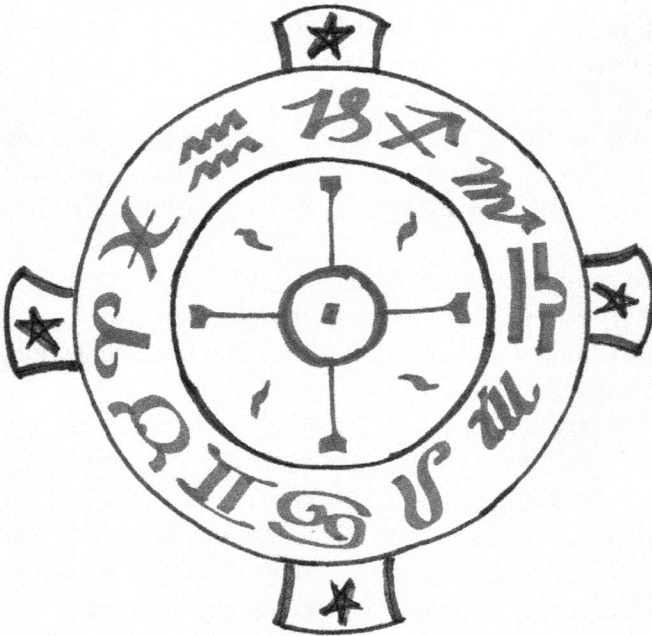

Seal of The Occult

(Traditional)

To help one obtain knowledge of ancient and arcane lore.

Scribe the Seal on parchment on a Night of Saturn, as Luna waxes in a Water Sign.

As the Seal is being scribed, chant over it, at least 15 times:

Ancient Spells and Wisdom from of yore,
these things do I implore,
and more . . . .
Knowledge of the Arcana Aracanorum, Mysteries of the past
for my mind's open forum.

Anoint a black candle with Black Arts Oil and set it to burn standing upon the Seal.

Set a Meditation Incense to burn and deeply concentrate on the Seal and any question needing an answer.

Let whatever message come to you as it will.

Keep the Seal on the North wall of your Occult Library.

TALISMAN OF THE SEVEN SEALS

(Traditional)

The power of the "Mystic Seven Planets of the Ancients."

It takes a full Week to properly make this Talisman. Begin to scribe it on a Day of Sol, Moon waxing in a Fire Sign, by making the Seal of the Sun.

Thereafter, each following day, scribe the Seal for the Planet of that Day.

Then consecrate it by passing it 6 times through the smoke of Frankincense and placing it under a lit 7 Color Candle in glass, on the following Day of Sol.

After the candle has burned itself out, carry the Talisman on your person to attract the positive forces of the Planets.

SEAL OF LUNA

A Moon Talisman is designed to attract the peaceful emotions into personal relationships and establish harmony in the domestic situation when made and consecrated on a Night of Luna as She waxes in a Water Sign.

It may also serve to cloud the mind and weave illusions of uncertainty for an enemy when made on the same night as Luna wanes in a Water Sign.

Scribe the Seal on parchment in inks of violet, gray and cobalt blue. Pass it 9 times through the smoke of Jasmine or Gardenia Incense as you chant:

Luna, Luna, Bona Fortuna, weave thy mystic spell of reflection
upon my wish without rejection.
Calm with peace or cloud with mist,
as I commune with thee in this Ancient tryst.

Meditate on the purpose for the Seal until it is felt it has absorbed the mental charge.

Then carry it on your person to work its intention.

SEAL OF MARS

A Talisman to take the offensive and destroy the work or Will of an enemy. Scribe on parchment on a Night of Mars as Luna waxes in a Fire Sign, in inks of red, golden yellow, orange and black.

To act as a shield of defense and ward off magical attacks from enemies, scribe on a Night of Mars, as Luna wanes in an Earth Sign.

Scribe the reason for making the Seal on the reverse side and anoint it with Mars Oil.

Pass the Seal five times through the smoke of Dragons Blood Reed Incense mixed with ground Stinging Nettles with these words:

God of war and warrior strong, offence against an evil throng. To fight my cause and win the day, up Mars, up I say!

or:

Shield of strength, defense of power, keep me safe from this hour.
Ward off the attacks of my ugly foe. I stand firm forever, let them know!

As an offensive weapon, it must be buried at or near the enemy's door step on a Night of Mars, Luna waxing.

As a defense, keep the Seal folded in the left shoe when the enemy is afoot and around about.

SEAL OF MERCURY

To gain acclaim in the fields of communications, acting, music or the performing arts. To help clarify one's own thinking and mental abilities, to sharpen the wit. A Psychic's Charm.

Scribe the Seal on a Night of Mercury as Luna waxes in a Water Sign with inks of yellow, blue, purple and black.

To confuse someones thinking and foul up lines of communication, scribe it on a Mercury Night as Luna wanes in an Air or Water Sign.

Carry the Seal in a yellow Charm Bag with Marjoram (Dittany of Crete), a small vial of Quicksilver and 8 pinches of Dill Seed, to attract the positive mercurial benefits.

Burn the Seal and scatter the ashes to the Four Winds to act as an aid in influencing the mind of others.

Consecrate the Seal on the proper nights of Mercury, as above, with a mixture of Storax, Olibanum and Benzoin as an Incense, by passing it 8 times through the smoke as these words are spoken:

Air Sprites and Sylphs and Spirits of Hermes, attend to me on wings of air!
Aid my psychic power and influence, bring the matters of mind to bear.

Silently meditate on the reason for the Talisman until it is felt to be sufficiently charged.

SEAL OF JUPITER

Scribe the Seal in inks of blue and purple on a night of Jupiter as the Moon waxes in an Earth Sign to help a project or circumstance expand and prosper. It is a good fortune seal for all constructive purposes.

Scribe on a Night of Jupiter as the Moon wanes in a water Sign to cause situations to deflate and dwindle away. Give it as a gift to an enemy.

Compose an Incense of Cinnamon, Cloves, Lavender and Benzoin to burn on charcoal and light a candle of royal blue or dark green, anointed with Jupiter Oil.

Pass the Seal four times through the smoke and say:

Zeus, the royal God of Wealth, preserves my money, peace and health.

or:

All expansion doth here halt, an afflicted Jupiter be at fault!

Set the Seal to rest beneath the candle until It burns itself out. If made for positive ends, carry it on your person.

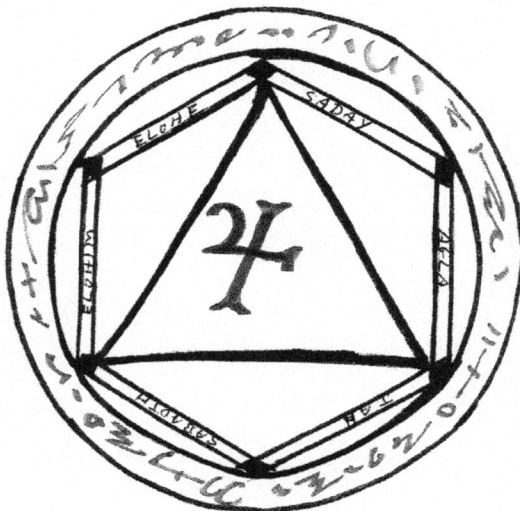

SEAL OF VENUS

To help increase love and friendship and attract the attention of a loved one, scribe this Seal on a Night of Venus, as Luna waxes in a Water or Earth Sign. Use inks of pink, green and copper brown.

Scribe the name of the intended Lover on the reverse of the Seal and set it to rest between two candles; one pink and the other green, anointed with a Love Drawing Oil.

Burn an Incense of Rose and/or Jasmine with some Sandalwood.

Set seven copper pennies in a circle around the candles and Seal, as these words are spoken:

Seven coins of copper, seven nights of love, seven times seven times seven times seven.
Such joy in life from the Seventh Heaven.

Let the candles burn themselves out and contrive to sew the rolled up Seal into the hem of the intended Lover's garment.

SEAL OF SATURN

In inks of black and purple, on a Night of Saturn, as Luna wanes in an Earth Sign, scribe this Seal to impede and restrict the actions and affairs of an enemy.

Pass it through the smoke of Patchouli and Valerian burned on coals. Set it beside a black candle anointed with Black Arts Oil and light the candle to burn slowly.

Speak not a word, but vision the bindings you would impose on the victim, as the candle burns.

Place the Seal and the candle stub, along with Knot Grass and Snake Root on the victim's door step at the Dark of the Moon.

Seal of Sol

For Good Luck, Good Fortune, Health and general Well-being, scribe this Seal in inks of red, yellow, gold and orange, on a Day of Sol as Luna waxes in a Fire or Earth Sign.

Pass the Seal 6 times through the smoke of Frankincense and 6 times through the flame of a gold candle anointed with Prosperity Oil.

Speak these words:

Wealth, good fortune and all life's blessing,
Sol will give for sure without guessing.
Prosperity and finances within my gate.
Sol will deflect all jealousy and hate.

Let the candle and incense burn out with the Seal beside them. Then place the Seal where the rays of the Sun will fall on it for six days in a row. Carry it on your person as a luck charm.

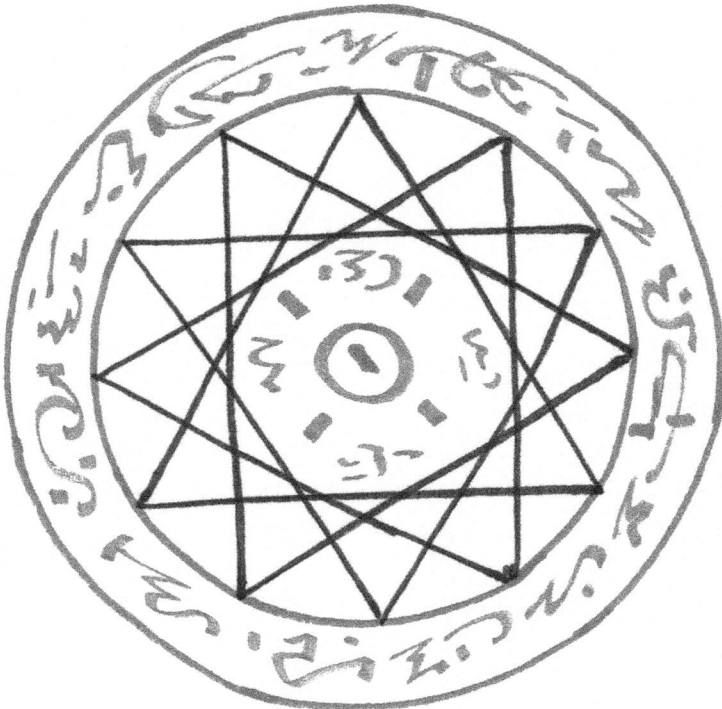

THE BASIC ROBE

This. is the basic way for the Probationer, aspiring to become a Craftsman First Degree, to make a simple robe which is worn in the process of the Ordeal to Craftsman status.

The reason for this robe, is to also help the Probationer in his/her discipline. He/she should be familiar with the old way of doing things.

An object made by hand carries the magnetic energy and charge of its maker. Therefore, a magical robe, where each stitch drawn by hand is pulled with an invocation and ritual intention, becomes a potent tool in the Witch's armory. It becomes more than just a robe for dress-up, but a part of the Witch's persona.

This may or may not be the type of formal Coven Robe. required by the Coven Council for Sabbat Ceremonies, Esbat Works and/or any other ceremony demanding robed attire.

This is the type of robe worn by those of Craftsman status. It does not have a hood.

When Craftsman is called to become a Covener, however, he/she must then buy or make the uniform type of robe with the Coven Insignia as required by the determinations of the Coven Council. Such would have a hood. The Formal Robe would always be black.

Coveners of all degrees, thereafter, during ceremonies of a formal nature, attend in robe with hoods up drawn to hang and drape the eyes. The person is only recognized by the color of his/her cinch cord and the proper grade sign given by hand (see next section).

The Summoner, standing at the entrance to the Magic Circle will see to it that only those showing the proper grade sign of their status and giving the right Watchword will be admitted to the Coven Circle. (The Watchword is determined each Hallowmas as part of the group ritual divination. This word embodies the Coven orientation for the year ahead. See *Book III*.)

There are three easy steps for making this basic robe:

Underside of material

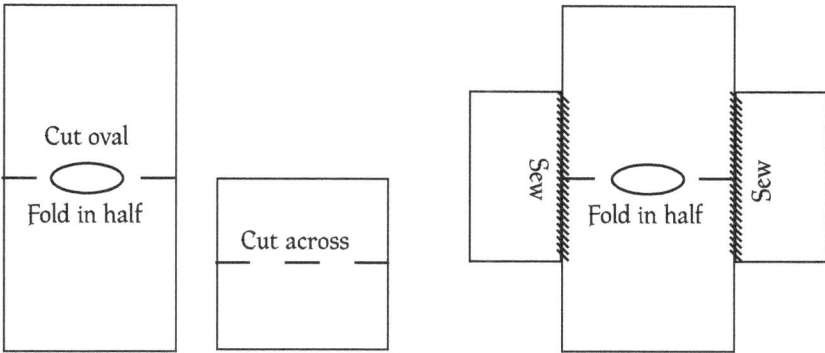

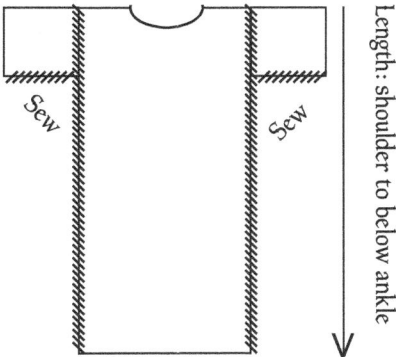

Cut oval

Fold in half

Cut across

Sew

Sew

Fold in half

Sew

Sew

Length: shoulder to below ankle

1. Two pieces of cloth; 1 piece is half the length of the other. Cut the oval for the head and cut the smaller piece for the sleeves.

2. Sew the two smaller pieces to the larger one.

3. Fold the robe and sew up the sides and sleeves. Turn inside out.

Sewing chant:

"I sew, I make, I make, I sew.
Sew and make, sew and make,
a robe of art for my Magic's sake."

THE CINGULUM OR CINCH CORD

The cinch Cord is of dyed leather, or cords of natural substances tied and braided together forming the belting for the ceremonial robe.

It should be hand made, either by the candidate for Initiation him/herself, or by others in the Coven for him/her as a gift.

Three strands of cording are required to make the Cinch Cord. They should be all of equal length, at least six feet long.

Three ends are knotted together and the strands carefully braided with this chant as each weaving is drawn:

Wrought by hand, this braided strand,
to show my Grade when Magic is made.

Each status in the Craft has its own color of Cingulum:

Craftsman 1st Degree, blue..

Covener 1st Degree, green.

Artisan 2nd Degree, yellow

Prac./HM 3rd Degree, red

High Priest 4th Degree, gold

High Priestess 5th Degree, silver

Elders 5th Degree, black.

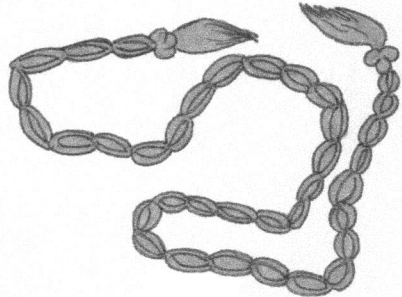

Prior to each person assuming a Degree or status in the Craft, the proper Cinch Cord/Cingulum must be made and brought to the Initiation Ceremony. It will be girded around the Initiate as part of the Declaration of Status by the Initiator. (See *Initiation Rituals, Book II*).

CRAFT GRADE SIGNS OF RANK

Upon entrance into the Ritual Chamber, or Circle for worship or Magical Ceremonies at the Covenstead, the Summoner will challenge all persons to show his/her grade sign. (Neophytes and Probationers excepted, as they have none and are only admitted by the Summoner and Sponsor at their respective Initiations.)

As each grade sign is shown, the Summoner will give a slight bow to those of higher rank than him/herself. To all he/she will say:

Only Perfect Love and Perfect Trust abide in this House.
What say ye?

To which the one entering will respond: *Blessed be.*

The Summoner will then require the Watchword to be whispered into his/her ear. Only thereupon will he/she step aside to allow the person to proceed into the Ritual Chamber or Circle.

No Covener should show irritation or impatience with the duty of the Summoner. This is to insure that only proper Coveners and those of true rank in the Craft participate in Craft works.

Visitors and those from other Traditions who have the right to attend Sabbat and/or Esbat, must be told the Watchword in order to pass the. Summoner. Perhaps their system does not have grade signs.

The Summoner has the right to forbid entrance to even those of V^0 status if such are not familiar with the Coven's Watchword. No Summoner should be afraid to enforce this rule.

The security of Craft Meetings is his/her particular domain.

The Signs:

Craftsman I^0: Fingers entwined, the index fingers extended to form a steeple; the thumbs forming the closed door.

Covener I^0: The same, except the thumbs are crossed, left over right for a female, and right over left for a male.

Artisan II^0: Right hand over heart, left hand held high as the Torch of Knowledge.

Practicus/Hand Maiden III°: Slight bow from the waist, forearms extended with palms up; Egyptian Servant Gesture.

High Priest IV°: Thumbs entwined, fingers of both hands extended and laid upon breast; The Phoenix asending.

High Priestess IV°: A triangle formed with the two hands pointing downward over the abdomen; the Water Symbol.

Magister Sacrorum V°: Right arm pointing upward, left arm out pointing earthward; the Tarot Magus.

Queen Mother V°: Both hands under breasts lifting upward; the Many Breasted Diana.

Philosophus V°: A triangle made with the two hands pointing upward upon the forehead; the Fire Symbol.

Oracle V°: Both hands held up concealing the eyes to show that an Oracle is for all without partiality.

EPILOGUE

Here we have a complete Occult Lodge System for the Craft of Wicca in practicing the Old Religion. It follows the Initiate throughout life from birth to death, giving all necessary rites and ceremonies, both major and minor, for a rising on the planes of being and aiming the Initiate on the Road of Adepthood.

It is a complete way of life for the Wicca and would require a dedicated life's work to accomplish the entire system.

It is a complete path of occult attainment for those seeking spiritual advancement in affecting the Great Work for Self-transformation.

It is not for everyone, nor does the system itself maintain that it is the only way, but it offers a path toward Occult Adepthood which is not complicated, nor abstruse, as some other systems, but difficult requiring sincere effort.

It has been offered for those who feel they can profit and gain thereby, in advancing the Self on the path of esoteric Wisdom. It holds up an ideal for the individual and/or group to strive for and embody as best as they are able.

If the ideas and organizational methods recommended by the Sacred Pentagraph are able to assist and give deeper insight in the Coven and initiatory aspects of the Old Religion, this work is well served.

- Finis -
This is my legacy for the Craft.
Blessed Be!
Tarostar